EFFEMINATE BELONGING

This book explores popular media narratives, queer theory, and biological explorations to coin a multifaceted understanding of effeminacy, gender normativity, and sexual pleasure. Moving from autobiographical narratives to twink porn, and well beyond, Richard Vytniorgu weaves together diverse voices while retaining a notably enjoyable authorial tone throughout; one committed to honoring the complexities of gay male bottoming and its cultural framings.
—Susanna Paasonen, *Professor of Media Studies, University of Turku, Finland*

What if the bottom is more than a sexual position? In Effeminate Belonging, *Richard Vytniorgu challenges readers to reconceptualize and reorient themselves towards and about the bottom. Drawing on an expansive archive that braids together the social sciences and literary and cultural studies, the bottom is no longer just a position, but an identity, one rich with complexity and nuance. By reimagining the idea of the bottom, masculinity and belonging is brought into a new light, one which illuminates possibility.*
—Jonathan A. Allan, *Professor and Canada Research Chair in Men and Masculinities, Faculty of Arts, Brandon University, Canada*

The uncoupling of same-sex desire, receptive positionality, and effeminacy might have enhanced the acceptance of same-sex sexuality and promoted the respectability of the LGBTQ+ community. Nevertheless, this separation has come at the expense of marginalizing men whose identities are shaped by these very aspects. This book presents a genuine and daring interdisciplinary argument for the reassessment and recognition of individuals embodying these characteristics. It advocates for the rehabilitation of fairies, pansies, and queens, while urging a more profound exploration of gender and positionality-based identities.
—Theo Sandfort, *Professor of Clinical Sociomedical Science (in Psychiatry), Department of Psychiatry, Columbia University, USA*

Breathtaking in scope and beautifully composed, Effeminate Belonging *illustrates the ways gay bottoms are structured as a*

'minority within a minority' and how fem gay bottoms write themselves into spaces of belonging despite these minoritizing tendencies. Richard Vytniorgu's interdisciplinary approach to the subject of fem gay bottoms and his deft negotiation of non-Western cultural practices to critique Anglo-American discourses of bottoming is revelatory. A model approach for research and a gift to clinicians, Effeminate Belonging *should be required reading for anyone interested in gay male identity or sexuality.*
—Timothy Oleksiak, *Associate Professor and Director of the Professional and New Media Writing Programme, Department of English, University of Massachusetts Boston, USA*

Drawing from multiple disciplines, including psychology, sociology, queer theories, porn studies and fiction literature, this book is extraordinarily well-researched in spotlighting the often dismissed populations of effeminate gay bottoms. Richard Vytniorgu thoroughly explores the nuanced in-between space of sexual orientations, gender nonconformity and sex role preference, highlighting the double marginalisation of homophobia and femmephobia, as well as courageously bringing forth the unsettling discussion on heterogender homosexuality. Vytniorgu skilfully analyses the narratives of sexuality, gender and sexual behaviours in Western culture and beyond, helping his readers with an in-depth understanding of the bio-psycho-social landscape in which effeminate gay bottoms live. It is an essential read for academics in psychology, sociology, and queer theories as well as psychotherapists specialising in gender, sex, and relationship diversity.
—Silva Neves, *Psychosexual and Relationship Psychotherapist and Author of* Sexology: The Basics, *Pink Therapy Clinical Associate, UK*

Richard Vytniorgu has marshalled his scholarly acumen and media savvy to investigate a pocket of gay male experience that is under-researched. The search for community as a fem gay bottom requires persistence, patience, self-compassion, and the courage to prize difference over conformity. The overlap of gender identity,

erotic practice, and embodied expression can present in different ways, and the author makes a thoughtful case for the meaningful link between effeminate belonging and sexual wellbeing.
—Don Shewey, *Author of* **The Paradox of Porn: Notes on Gay Male Sexual Culture and Daddy Lover God: A Sacred Intimacy Journey**

EFFEMINATE BELONGING

Gender Nonconforming Experience and Gay Bottom Identities

BY

RICHARD VYTNIORGU
University of Hertfordshire, UK

United Kingdom – North America – Japan – India
Malaysia – China

Emerald Publishing Limited
Emerald Publishing, Floor 5, Northspring, 21-23 Wellington Street, Leeds LS1 4DL

First edition 2024

Copyright © 2024 Richard Vytniorgu.
Published under exclusive licence by Emerald Publishing Limited.

Reprints and permissions service
Contact: www.copyright.com

No part of this book may be reproduced, stored in a retrieval system, transmitted in any form or by any means electronic, mechanical, photocopying, recording or otherwise without either the prior written permission of the publisher or a licence permitting restricted copying issued in the UK by The Copyright Licensing Agency and in the USA by The Copyright Clearance Center. Any opinions expressed in the chapters are those of the authors. Whilst Emerald makes every effort to ensure the quality and accuracy of its content, Emerald makes no representation implied or otherwise, as to the chapters' suitability and application and disclaims any warranties, express or implied, to their use.

British Library Cataloguing in Publication Data
A catalogue record for this book is available from the British Library

ISBN: 978-1-80455-010-6 (Print)
ISBN: 978-1-80455-009-0 (Online)
ISBN: 978-1-80455-011-3 (Epub)

INVESTOR IN PEOPLE

CONTENTS

Preface ix
Acknowledgements xi

Introduction 1
Notes on Terminology 17
Notes on Research Ethics 19

Part 1: Theories, Perspectives and Sources
1. Gender Nonconformity, Effeminacy and Gay Bottom Identities 23
2. Marginalisation and Belonging 41
3. Narratives on the Margins 57

Part 2: Readings, Concerns and Directions
4. Fem Gay Bottom: Can I Be All Three? 69
5. Fem Bottoms in Practice 93
6. Effeminate Belonging and Sexual Wellbeing 115
Conclusion 125

About the Author 129
Bibliography 131
Index 151

PREFACE

All the time, I think, we want to find out about each other, to know if we really belong to each other, belong together.
(Bartlett, 1988, p. xx)

These words by the novelist Neil Bartlett capture the essence of what this book is about. At the height of the AIDS crisis, he wanted to know if he belonged with Oscar Wilde. In the late 1980s, very few wanted to belong with gay men, and an entire generation of gay men risked being wiped out.

While issues of belonging may have seemed especially pertinent to gay men at the time I was born, as the 1980s turned into the 1990s, they are also relevant now, as indeed they were before the 1990s. Many gay men grow up feeling different from other men. This is especially so if they present in ways others would deem gender nonconforming or effeminate, or in ways that deviate from socially normative standards of masculinity. And this in turn is connected to perceptions and self-awareness concerning sexual role and behaviour, particularly bottoming, or engaging in receptive anal intercourse with men.

Fears around anal sex have always been central to homophobic and effeminophobic attitudes, especially in countries such as Britain that at various times carried punitive legislation targeted specifically at male–male anal sex, or 'sodomy'. Up until the Offences Against the Person Act 1861, men in England, Wales and Ireland risked the death penalty if caught engaging in 'the detestable and abominable vice of buggery', as the Buggery Act 1533 described anal sex. And, until the Sexual Offences Act 2003, it was technically illegal for men in public to 'importune' one another for consensual sex with each other, as it was for schools to even talk about gay sex with pupils, through Clause/Section 28. In many other places around the world, anal sex between men – hence bottoming – is still illegal, and in some instances punishable by death.

The impact of cumulative prejudice against gay anal sex, bottoming and effeminacy on males throughout history cannot be overstated. It can still be a conscious task to belong with these non-normative aspects of self in contexts that hold very different standards of what is deemed typical or normal when it comes not only to being an adult male but being gay as well.

Effeminate Belonging is about the stories and experiences of male–male sex and love at the edges of acceptability: about those who are fem and who bottom and who see these two aspects as inextricably connected in themselves despite wider resistance to such a synergy. Perhaps because of this connection, this book is about the challenge of belonging in the gay community, with its own shifting norms and prejudices, as much as it is about belonging in the wider world.

As I will argue, the best response to this challenge of belonging is not to pretend – as some gay men do – that bottoming has nothing to do with effeminacy or gender nonconformity, now or in the past, or that bottoming should be analysed independently of gender expression. Rather, I argue for the need to forge more inclusive attitudes towards those for whom this connection feels both natural and integral to their sense of self, even if this goes against the political grain. Given the centrality of anal sex and non-normative gender expression to anti-gay sentiment throughout history, it seems crucial that the voices of those for whom bottoming and effeminacy go hand in hand are given sustained scholarly attention.

Since beginning to write about these topics and connecting on social media with fem bottoms from a diversity of places, I've found that far from being considered peripheral, self-indulgent or irrelevant, issues of belonging rooted in gender expression, sexual orientation and anal sex role preference are integral to some gay men's wellbeing:

- 'I like how you explore bottomness as an identity and not just a sexual practice. And that you bring up the bond that we effeminate bottoms share. Like a sisterhood of pussyboys.'
- 'Your research shows that feminine bottoms exist and we are here.'
- 'I think you are doing something wonderful for this particular section of the gay community.'
- 'What you do is brave, cool and encouraging for boys like me.'

These comments, which come from around the world, speak of a desire to belong, to know that one is not alone. It's in this spirit that I offer this book to various people: to other academics; to LGBTQ+, health, and educational professionals; to artists and activists; and perhaps most importantly, to those like me who knew they were different, but couldn't articulate why, and why it mattered.

I hope this book can begin to help in this process of articulation, and in so doing, to re-orient perceptions of what it might mean to be gay and belong.

Abergavenny, 29 February 2024

ACKNOWLEDGEMENTS

My special thanks go to Arnold Zwicky for seeing in me what I couldn't myself, and to Jaime Garcia-Iglesias, Timothy Oleksiak and Robert Jacobsson for their shared belief in the importance of research on bottoms and bottoming.

Thanks to Jean-Philippe Imbert and David O'Mullane for organising the Sex Panics Conference at Dublin City University in October 2023, where I received encouragement and feedback that has helped galvanise this project in its final stages.

To all those who have reached out to me via Twitter/X: thank you. It means more than I can say to hear that my work has helped, inspired and encouraged you in your own self-explorations.

I would like to thank Heike Bartel, who not only introduced me to Emerald through her book on eating disorders in men but who also showed me how to use the study of autobiographical writing to understand and enhance personal and social wellbeing.

My thanks also go to the institutions that gave me the impetus and space to work on this project: the University of Exeter, University of Hertfordshire, the Wellcome Trust, the Arts and Humanities Research Council and the Economic and Social Research Council.

Finally, I would also like to thank the team at Emerald for assisting me, and to the three anonymous peer reviewers who gave such helpful and encouraging feedback.

INTRODUCTION

Men who primarily engage in receptive anal sex with men, often known as *bottoms*, and who are also perceived to be and/or self-identify as effeminate, fem or gender nonconforming face multiple challenges when it comes to navigating their identities and sense of belonging in the wider gay community and beyond. Males who are perceived to be insufficiently masculine, and who prefer to be receptive in anal sex with men, are frequently considered undesirable as sexual and romantic partners. Such males are also criticised by those in the gay community for perpetuating unhelpful and inaccurate stereotypes about gay men (Thoma et al., 2021). Many gay men would argue that being a bottom shouldn't automatically be equated with being effeminate or unmanly (O'Flynn, 2018). For too long, some would insist, have gay men, and bottoms in particular, fought to be recognised *as real men* (Milton, 2022). By this logic, being fucked by a man needn't necessitate a specific gender expression or even a specific identity. It's just something you *do*.

This book is in sympathy with such an argument and recognises that for many gay men in the West – predominantly Western Europe and North America, but also Australia and New Zealand – *bottom* is merely a temporary sex position which in no way indicates an absence of masculinity. For many gay men, bottoming is often coupled with topping (being the fucker rather than the fucked) as part of a versatile sex life, and indeed it may well be the case that anal sex is excluded from an individual's sexual practice altogether.

The dominant climate in LGBTQ+ media in the West seems to support the notion that anal sex role should be separated from stereotypical gender expression, as part of a progressive politics set against heteronormativity. Such a culture celebrates the existence of fem dom tops, masc power bottoms, versatile men who 'flip fuck' and even *sides* who eschew anal sex and may prefer oral sex or mutual masturbation (Bollas, 2023; Kort, 2020).

But this book is not primarily about such men. *Effeminate Belonging* is about males who are now on the margins of mainstream gay life in the West. I want to highlight the experiences and vantage points of those males who are gender nonconforming and who are also strongly associated – in fantasy and/or in real life – with taking the bottom position in anal sex with men.

Indeed, they are so identified with this as their primary mode of sexual behaviour that they are happy to identify as bottoms or even as effeminate or fem bottoms (or similar terms in their own language).

In some cases, such bottoms may even shy away from self-identifying as men even if they still see themselves as male and actively seek and desire masculinity and manhood in the men they choose as partners. Thus, for them, *bottom* is an identity as much as a sexual practice, to the point where even if one has never been anally penetrated, one can still identify as a bottom. Crucially, such males see their gender expression as intricately connected to their sexual preferences in ways that other gay men would strongly resist.

In a different historical moment, and even today in some non-Western localities, such a combination of gender expression and anal sex role preference would hardly be considered unusual, although it may be stigmatised and result in varying degrees of marginalisation. The key distinguishing factor for these same-sex attracted males is that they do not simply bottom: they *are* bottoms, and somehow recognise that their sexuality is of a different order to that of the men they typically find sexually attractive as partners. As anthropologist Don Kulick has argued:

> *...whether they are the* mahus, hijras, kathoeys, xaniths, *or* berdaches *of non-Western societies, or the mollies and fairies of our own history, links between habitual receptivity in anal sex and particular effeminate behavioral patterns structure the ways in which males who are regularly penetrated are perceived, and they structure the ways in which many of those males think about and live their lives.* (Kulick, 1998, p. 575)

The fact that there have been and still are words in non-Anglophone languages to describe precisely the kind of combination of anal sex role and gender expression denoted by the contemporary English label *fem gay bottom* suggests that this is a transcultural and indeed transhistorical phenomenon, but one that has receded from view in recent years. Attention to non-Western forms is needed to properly contextualise the Western effeminate bottom.

It's one of the major premises of this book that non-Western labels, often working-class and colloquial, as well as some Western labels which are also working-class and colloquial, encapsulate a broadly equivalent transcultural and transhistorical combination of effeminate gender expression, with varying degrees of flamboyance and with or without cross-dressing, and receptive sex role or being a bottom in anal sex with masculine men (Murray, 2000; Norton, 2016). Those who have been assigned these labels or who self-identify as them need not adhere strictly to these ideal types, and there is some flexibility around the nature of the connection and the power dynamics they connote. But they do so sufficiently and in public view to fall into these personality categories and modes of self-awareness, even if eventually they may change preferences or discard such identification over their 'sexual career', depending on the current partner or stage of life (Murray, 1995).

It's also true that these ideal types can, in some instances, become prisons in which same-sex attracted men often feel compelled to place themselves simply to indicate to others their sexual preference and availability for the same sex (Loftin, 2007; Murray, 2000). For example, studies have shown that after migrating to the West, or indeed even simply by adopting a contemporary gay identity, some men who previously assumed a traditionally effeminate, sexually passive role have left this behind in favour of a more congenial versatile and more masculine self-presentation – in Latin American discourses historically called *moderno* or *internacional*, or, as simply *gay* (Carrillo & Fontdevila, 2014; Guasch, 2011). Similarly, during and after the Second World War, middle-class homosexuals in Britain and the homophile movement in the United States increasingly detached gender expectations from sexual orientation in an attempt to claim social respectability and acceptance as masculine men, in the process distancing themselves from working-class effeminate *queens, fairies, pansies, poofs* and *swishes* (Chauncey, 1994; Loftin, 2007; Norton, 2016).

This transformation can, of course, be interpreted as breaking the oppressive power dynamics of a patriarchal, heterosexist and heteronormative environment in which the only possible combination of sexual complementarity is a powerful man and a disempowered sexual receptacle – a female, or a receptive male who has lost all pretence at being a man. For such men, entering a more egalitarian relationship with another man in which both males are considered men and, in theory, both able to top and bottom (or do neither), would be an act of liberation from oppressive norms and power structures (Nguyen, 2014). As Wayne Wooden and Jay Parker argue in their classic, *Men Behind Bars: Sexual Exploitation in Prison* (1983), 'a positive gay identity attempts to free men from the tyranny of rigid role-playing' – a rigidity which is, these authors argue, 'directly opposed to the goals of the modern gay movement' (p. 145).

This argument is further developed in Walt Odets's *Out of the Shadows: Reimagining Gay Men's Lives* (2020), in which the 'gay sensibility' should symbolise the triumph of egalitarian relational dynamics between men and, ultimately, a versatile sex life. For Odets, some exclusive or 'total' tops and bottoms might be in accord with their 'entire conscious internal sensibilities', but others – perhaps even most – are containing 'aspects of their unconscious sensibilities that might, if recognized and allowed expression, nurture a broader, a more authentic experience' (p. 54). For Odets, 'polarized' relationships 'fortunately [...] do not describe all Americans, particularly today's younger, educated, urban adults' (p. 39). But to my mind, it's also possible that making the meaning of gay synonymous with masculinity and sexual versatility is just as much an attempt at social control as the 'inauthentic' polarised forms of masculine-effeminate complementarity for which Odets reserves his scorn.

For some males, adopting or retaining a form of heterogender homosexuality (masc–fem as opposed to masc–masc or fem–fem) would, paradoxically, represent an act of liberation and entrance into something more authentic. For such fem bottoms, the egalitarian, versatile and masculinist model has now become, for them, an oppressive, inauthentic norm and for whom the internet offers a plethora of creative ways to negotiate heterogender sexual identities and seek masculine 'total top' sexual partners who, in their own ways, may also be tiring of the 'gold standard' of egalitarian sexual versatility monopolising meanings of being gay (Vytniorgu, 2024a). Thus, the attempt to universalise a North American or Western European gay sexual politics as being ethically better and more psychologically fulfilling – for all gay men – presents serious problems, not only for non-Western and global majority settings in which *gay* has limited appeal or reach but for those within the West who do not identify with the kind of 'blended' sensibility so praised by Odets.

In the contemporary Anglophone-speaking West, identity names are not readily at hand to describe those males who prefer to bottom in anal sex with other men and who are also gender nonconforming, and, crucially, who see these two aspects of themselves as mutually reinforcing, strongly influencing their overall sense of self. To be sure, in 1972, American scholars still referred to *queen* as an 'effeminate homosexual' who 'prefer[s] more masculine men' (Farrell, 1972, p. 106) or, in 1984, as a 'passive, effeminate homosexual' with a distinct personality type and interest in masculine or even hypermasculine male sexual and romantic partners (Person & Ovesey, 1984, p. 173).[1] And, out of all the possible historical Anglophone words available that might still connote a fem gay bottom whose identity encompasses more than simply their sexual behaviour/preferences, *queen* is possibly the closest term at hand, however imprecise its usage may be in practice.[2]

Beyond *queen*, there simply aren't many words available to describe this combination, perhaps due to the relentless attempts among Odets's urban, educated gay men to eliminate any suggestion that effeminacy and being sexually receptive have any intrinsic connection. And it's this reality which, I would argue, contributes to feelings of disconnect and marginalisation in contemporary Western settings, where it's largely inadmissible to suggest that being a bottom is in any way responsive to or connected to being gender nonconforming or effeminate – terms which themselves demand greater scrutiny and which are explored in detail in Chapter 1.

This book therefore aims to explore the interconnections between sex object choice (being attracted to men), sex role (being a bottom) and gender expression (being gender nonconforming or effeminate), arguing that negotiating these different facets of the self has implications for feelings of marginalisation and belonging. The book proceeds by reading contemporary Western lived experience narratives in a range of media, exploring gender nonconforming experience and bottom identities in their broadest remit, by connecting these two to a critical mass of multidisciplinary literature on these themes, and by contextualising them through reference to non-Western parallels which, while not completely equivalent, nevertheless reveal striking similarities that help to refine the key areas of debate concerning effeminate belonging in the West. In doing so, this book recognises that 'comparative studies across time and across social systems are a vital prerequisite to the emergence of a satisfactory concept of human homosexual behavior in all its fullness and complexity' (Dynes, 1995, n.p.).

One of the deeper aims of the book is to begin to consider gendered and sexual belonging in more inclusive and dialogic ways. I want to try and move beyond an *us and them* mentality in which self-identified LGBTQ+ people set themselves in opposition to non-LGBTQ+ people in an understandable but separatist way – often mirroring the treatment they have received at the hands of non-LGBTQ+ people. I am interested in exploring modes of effeminate belonging in digital and non-digital spaces and places typically made up of a range of different people. To what extent do the narratives emphasise the necessity for withdrawal from such places in favour of a metropolitan gay or LGBTQ+ enclave immured from the rest of society? I am interested in how reconciliation might begin to take place, between those who have experienced prejudice and violence at the hands of others in different places and spaces, and those in such spaces who have, for whatever reason, decided that a *faggot, tapette, queen, bicha*, etc., does not belong there.

One of the main reasons for including non-Western and global majority narratives and perspectives in this book – especially those from working-class contexts in which 'global gay' or LGBTQ+ politics has limited appeal or reach or is hybridised with local forms – is that they show, however imperfectly, that 'non-normative' individuals can belong with others in non-oppositional and generative ways. And, moreover, that it's possible, if often challenging and painful, to share the same space in ways that promote a bottom-up (no pun intended), day-to-day awareness of difference at the *I-thou* level. In the West, this has certainly been the case in the past, even in interwar south and east London, as Matt Houlbrook has deftly shown: working-class *queans* were 'acknowledged, precariously accepted, and often welcomed' by the rest of the local community (2005, p. 160), as they were also on merchant navy vessels well into the 1970s and 1980s, where queens took 'straight' husbands and effectively became wives on board (Baker & Stanley, 2003). How might examples like these be instructive today?

STATE OF THE FIELD

Current research in the area is alarmingly fragmented. In the humanities, work on effeminacy typically views the phenomenon through queer theory lenses that aim to emphasise the social construction of power dynamics that cast the effeminate as the queer 'other' to forms of hegemonic masculinity (Bristow, 1995; Hennen, 2008; Maddison, 2015). Scholarship on gay bottoms forms another field of research altogether, mostly from within the social sciences (Brooks et al., 2017; Hoppe, 2011), which explores identity formations and experiences of struggle, marginalisation, and stigma around bottoming – as well as power and pleasure (Hoppe, 2011; Moskowitz & Garcia, 2019). Within the humanities, work on the crucial intersections of bottoming and gender expression in media, film and other cultural texts is lacking, with some key exceptions which, while important in raising the visibility of the area as a necessary field of inquiry, can also be over-reliant on queer theory approaches to do the interpretive work.

Such work in the humanities also tends to overlook scientific research that also has explanatory power when it comes to understanding cultural representations of effeminacy and gay bottom identities and experiences (Allan, 2016; Geraths, 2022; Kemp, 2013; Nguyen, 2014; Oleksiak, 2022). Historically, research drawing on queer theory has typically dismissed any reference to transhistorical or transcultural 'essences' of same-sex self-awareness and personality and questions the use of scientific discourse in explaining sexual orientation and/or sex and gender. In this book I aim to demonstrate, however, that inquiry into sexual identities and experiences based on a sensitive reading of lived experience narratives can be strengthened by drawing on the insights of psychobiological studies in the human sciences.

Research in psychology is currently exploring gender nonconformity and anal sex role preference among gay men from a more psychobiological stance (Swift-Gallant et al., 2021; VanderLaan et al., 2022). This work, while still indicative, nevertheless suggests that bottoms experience more gender nonconformity than tops. Gender nonconformity in this literature is broadly equivalent to an effeminate gender expression and goes far beyond stereotypical representations of effeminacy associated with flamboyance. It's in this sense that I conflate the terms in this book; although there may be a case to be made for gender nonconformity signifying something broader than simply the manifestation of typically feminine traits in males – it could indicate a broader refusal to adhere to stereotypically masculine traits without necessarily leaning towards the feminine. However, due to the way in which the scientific literature has, and continues to use, the term *gender nonconformity* among males as a proxy for *effeminacy*, this book will maintain this terminological equivalence. Although, I am aware that this will not be a perfect synergy for all readers and that one might ideally speak of *effeminacies* rather than *effeminacy* (Hennen, 2001). I explore these questions in more detail in Chapter 1.

Contemporary psychological research on gender nonconformity and anal sex roles among gay men, bisexual men and men who have sex with men builds on a much older body of literature in sex research and lesbian and gay studies, published in journals such as *Archives of Sexual Behavior*, *Journal of Sex Research*, and *Journal of Homosexuality*. Some of this research has examined the endocrinological, immunological and genetic factors which are thought to shape or influence gender nonconforming and homosexual outcomes among boys and men (LeVay, 2017), while also establishing the relationship between gender nonconformity among boys and a homosexual orientation among men (Carrier, 1977; Hines, 2011; Li et al., 2017; Weinrich et al., 1992).

Much of this research has argued for a clear link between gender nonconforming experiences in childhood and later homosexual or bisexual identities, behaviours and preferences in men, while also stressing that effeminate experiences are only relevant for *some* gay men – by no means all – and that they may change or subside with an individual's own life course. A subsection of relevant research from a social scientific dimension has also sought to understand how and why adolescent males defeminise due to hormonal changes in puberty and/or to feel accepted among their peers and avoid the stigma of being identified by others as gay (Glick et al., 2007; Harry, 1983; Pascoe, 2012; Taywaditep, 2002).

This book aims to triangulate these related but atomised bodies of research and bring a much-needed interdisciplinary approach to the study of gender nonconforming experience and gay bottom identities, behaviours and preferences among males, anchored in an empathetic and sensitive reading of lived experience narratives in the cultural domain. Indeed, while valuing the work of empirical and psychobiological studies, I hope to show that positivist accounts of gender nonconformity and bottom identity and practice only tell half the story, and are often unconscious or inattentive to the emotional, embodied, and fraught ways in which individuals experience and represent themselves that often shine through in stories and other representational media.

Moreover, while I think it's important to recognise the variety of gay bottom identities out there, it would also be irresponsible, given the research that exists, to pretend that being a bottom has nothing to do with gender or can be analysed independently of this (Hoppe, 2011). Indeed, one of the key arguments of this book is that being both effeminate and a bottom has critical implications for feelings of marginalisation and belonging in the gay community and beyond. Many of the narratives explored in this book confront the experience of effeminophobia or femmephobia – the fear of femininity in males – and the association therefore not only with homosexuality, but with being fucked and a resultant loss of manhood (Hoskin, 2019; Richardson, 2009; Sedgwick, 1991). As Leo Bersani famously wrote, we are dealing with the 'intolerable image of a grown man, legs high in the air, unable to refuse the suicidal ecstasy of being a woman' (Bersani, 1987, p. 212).

Effeminate Belonging highlights the ways in which anxieties and desires around effeminate bottoms intersect with feelings of marginalisation and belonging in the home, family, school, healthcare settings, LGBTQ+ community, online and also in the body itself. As such, the book draws on work in geographies of sexualities which affirm that sexuality 'cannot be understood without understanding the spaces through which it is constituted, practised and lived' (Browne et al., 2009, p. 4; Bell & Valentine, 1995).

Mannerisms, voice and clothing have always been and still are key cultural markers of effeminacy and are routinely 'read' by people in different places and spaces as a proxy for homosexual identity formation (Norton, 2016). Research has shown the extent to which these signifiers are used to consolidate homosexual identities in others, sometimes with negative consequences which result in stereotyping (Daniele et al., 2020; Ravenhill & de Visser, 2017; Schofield & Schmidt, 2005). As I will show: voice, physical build, clothing and mannerisms act as features which shape preoccupations with effeminate belonging – with absorbing, making sense of, and eventually, belonging with gender nonconformity and sexual receptivity in different places and spaces.

Intended primarily for academics studying sex, gender and sexuality from multiple disciplinary angles in the humanities and social sciences, the book is also intended to be of use to LGBTQ+ practitioners and counsellors and other mental health, educational and sexual wellbeing professionals who work with gender nonconforming gay men and who are keen to understand the relationship between gender nonconformity and sex roles and their impact on a sense of wellbeing and belonging. The book highlights the value of the arts and new media, especially from an autobiographical stance, for exploring and enhancing the lived experiences of boys and men at the intersections of gender nonconformity and bottom identity and experience, in Western and global majority contexts.

The narratives under discussion are drawn from the margins of contemporary gay media and culture: from film, autobiographical documentaries, animation, music videos, photo narratives, online forums and microblogging sites, gay porn and written erotica. All are in the public domain, and in themselves reveal the extent of interest generated around themes of effeminacy, bottoms and the search for belonging faced by fem bottoms in the gay community; they are indeed a 'minority within a minority' (Reilly, 2016, p. 173).

AUTHOR POSITIONALITY

Few scholars studying gender and sexuality do so in a wholly detached and impersonal manner. In my case, I was in the same school year as singer and actor Olly Alexander (born 1990), whose documentary *Olly Alexander: Growing Up Gay* (2017) I discuss in Chapter 4. Many of Alexander's British school experiences resonate with my own, including the struggle to find others who are like you at a formative stage in your life, when experiences of bullying, ostracisation and feelings of difference and shame threaten to overwhelm. The search for belonging has been key for me ever since.

I always knew I was different from the other boys around me. As a boy, I liked dressing up in girls' clothes. I imitated and impersonated females, enjoyed wearing makeup and played with girls as well as with boys. I strongly identified with the women rather than the men in my life, and I wanted to get pregnant and become a mother when I was older. I hated rough-and-tumble play and boys' sports, and I shied away from talking sexually about girls with the boys around me because I was worried I didn't share their sexuality – their desire to penetrate. And they knew it, too. I was called a *poof* from early on in primary school (aged five or six), and throughout my early teenage years was repeatedly asked by the sporty, macho boys ('jocks') if I was gay. Why they asked me, I don't know: they had already decided on the answer – an answer I didn't like because I knew it was true.

The bullies would imitate limp wrists, a swishy walk and gay voice (with an emphasis on sibilant/s/sounds) as if to say: even if you deny it, you really *are* a poof. You aren't just gay: you're *obviously* gay. Other boys from other places might well have heard something similar, being called a *sissy, fag, tapette, bicha, bakla, marica, loca*, all with connotations of effeminacy and being sexually receptive, or becoming so as an adult.

In some ways, the bullies were right, somehow knowing that, as rhetoric scholar Timothy Oleksiak writes, 'bottoming is carried in the body' (2022, p. 358). I was all the things the bullies said I was, even as I tried (and failed) to be like them. But they could have been nicer in telling me I was unlike them. At times, the burden of those taunts was intolerable. As Andrew Powles has written in his memoir of being a 'dedicated bottom', growing up, other people 'had the naming rights': other boys 'recognized and labelled something in me before I had managed to articulate it' (2003, p. 112). In many ways, this book explores how we reclaim the 'naming rights' to ourselves, to reclaim what it means to be gay, fem, and a bottom, often by searching for a sense of belonging with others, even if that means imagining beyond our own time and culture and the places in which we find ourselves.

It's only in recent years that I realised I needn't have felt alone. During my adolescence, in my rather futile attempts to defeminise and become a 'normal' middle-class young man, I sought to belong with those who only had space for me if I aspired to the identities they sought for themselves. Not only did I block from my consciousness openly effeminate gay celebrities, but I eliminated gay figures entirely from my headspace. And yet, in my own cultural orbit and generation, I am flanked not only by Olly Alexander, but also by public figures such as diver and knitter Tom Daley (born 1994), weatherman, TV presenter, and drummer Owain Wyn Evans (born 1984), lifestyle YouTuber Nicolas Fairford (born 1990), singer, dancer, and actor Layton Williams (born 1994), and others – all of whom are openly gay and fem to varying degrees. These male figures, as well as an array of (younger) social media influencers, now represent visible public male points of reference for a younger generation of gender nonconforming gay male youth, who may be struggling to belong and questioning what being male means for them.

Does all this constitute a gay bottom identity? This is a key question, which I also explore in Chapter 1. As Raja Halwani has argued in relation to a 'homosexual identity', one can be homosexual without having a 'homosexual identity'. An identity in this instance is defined as something which 'goes a long way to shape the kind of person he or she is' (1998, p. 32).[3] Substituting 'bottom' for 'homosexual':

> ...to claim that I have a [bottom] identity is to claim, roughly, that my [bottomhood] plays a very important role in determining the kind of person I am: how it enters into my social, political, moral, emotional, and intellectual life. But it is entirely conceivable to have a person who is a [bottom] yet who has no [bottom] identity. (p. 32)

Gay bottom identities in this book encapsulate varying modes of self-awareness as sexually receptive with other men, and/or a related sense of being identified as such by others. Such identity formation varies from context to context, and even fluctuates within specific individuals and over time. And, of course, having a bottom identity in no way means that this is the sum of who you are as a person.

'Identity' is certainly an imperfect term, but it is a sufficient one, and one that ideally needs to be examined through the lens of narrative, for 'identity is that which emerges in and through narratives' (Hinchman & Hinchman, 2001, p. xviii). Or, as Cate Watson has argued, 'to the extent that all narratives of personal experience involve the positioning of self in relation to the other, all may be said to be concerned with identity' (Watson, 2012, p. 460). The book argues for the possibility and existence of sufficiently central aspects of the self that coalesce around sexual orientation, preferred sex role and gender expression, which contribute to a specific mode of self-awareness and relatedness to other people (Carrillo, 2002; Norton, 2016). And, moreover, that this self-awareness is refracted through narrative in a range of media that requires simultaneous attention to the texture of narrative and the texture of bottom identities.

METHODOLOGICAL CONSIDERATIONS

Author positionality thus raises methodological questions about *scientific enquiry* – a term which perhaps rightly is subjected to critique by some qualitative researchers and literary-cultural scholars (McKee, 2014). The key question is whether my own personal identification with the topic under consideration is likely to bias, distort or otherwise tamper with how I select, analyse and interpret the evidence used to develop my argument. If this was an empirical study aiming at a degree of reliability in method and generalisability of findings, then it would be prudent to scrutinise the extent to which authorial identification with the topic might make it difficult for others to 'go and do likewise'.

However, this study builds on a rich history of affective work in gender and sexuality studies, which is inspired by feminist epistemologies and questions the possibility and even desirability, in some lines of enquiry, of so-called academic neutrality, and which actively esteems the personal, subjective, emotive and embodied ways in which knowledge about gender and sexuality can occur in the arts and media (McKee, 2014; Paasonen, 2018). Critical practices of life narrative, autoethnography and feminist theory are just some of the ways in which scholars in the humanities and social sciences have humanised work on topics concerning gender and sexuality, often by privileging autobiographical engagement with the content under consideration and de-centring scientific discourses of analysis when it comes to engaging with people's creative and personal stories (Ahmed, 2017; Buchanan & Ryan, 2010; Oleksiak, 2022; Santoro, 2016).

Thinkers such as Parker Palmer and Michael Polanyi have emphasised the limits of objectivism and the importance, where possible, of interpersonal identification in the quest for knowledge, particularly in the humanities and social sciences: 'If what we know is an abstract, impersonal, apart from us, it cannot be truth, for truth involves a vulnerable, faithful, and risk-filled interpenetration of the knower and the known' (Palmer, 1993, p. 49).

Moreover, feminist-inspired critical writing has sought to experiment with forms of scholarly engagement that 'aim to remain open to surprises and uncertainties in processes of knowledge creation' (Paasonen, 2011, 2018, p. 29). Similarly, Oleksiak has wondered what it means to 'compose as a bottom': 'The rhetorical bottom extends bottoming into composing and delinks bottoming from its context as a sexual experience without losing traces of those meanings' (2022, pp. 358–359). Re-visiting the rhetorical concept of stance, Oleksiak affirms the bottom's stance as a 'receptive stance, an openness to the pleasures that are found in what is offered' (p. 360). To me, this seems like a courageous stance: to demonstrate openness in knowledge creation in ways that bring 'texts, ideas, and other people into [our]selves' as bottoms (p. 360). For a book on belonging, this act of bringing 'other people into ourselves' seems especially salient.

So when I draw on a range of knowledge bases to engage with the narratives under discussion in this book, I do so to broaden the interpretive possibilities while simultaneously highlighting the value of receptive and affective interpersonal engagement with the narratives and authors or content creators. I am interested in the distinctive kinds of knowledge – unique, emotional, embodied – that can arise from reading creative and autobiographical narratives alongside attention to wider scientific studies that exclude such readings from their remit (Bartel, 2020; Schleifer & Vannatta, 2019).

Embracing the visual and the moving image as well as the written text also invites consideration of how embodied affect and arousal intersect with and even overtake from reading when it comes to online imagery, especially the erotic and pornographic. As Susanna Paasonen has argued,

> *Using reading to describe the analytical work done in Internet research means bypassing the differences between text and still and moving images, the ways in which they play into each other on Web interfaces, and the ways that they are experienced and made sense of together, separately, and in hybrid ways. (2011, p. 14)*

Engaging with content in a range of media – written, visual, moving and still, online and offline – is also an invitation to understand how different selves are reflected, autobiographically, and how they are seen, touched, and read by others as a 'moving target, a set of self-referential practices', which also impact belonging with gendered and sexual identities (Smith & Watson, 2010, p. 1; see Chapter 3). As Chapter 5 suggests, arousal and visceral engagement – what Paasonen calls *carnal resonance* – seem crucial in opening ways to belong with and among fem bottoms, to 'find out if we really belong to each other, belong together', as Neil Bartlett says (2011; Bartlett, 1988, p. xx).

These epistemological considerations are especially pertinent to the specific work of engaging with sexually explicit material in the online era. As John Mercer explains in *Gay Pornography: Representations of Sexuality and Masculinity* (2017), any research that studies forms of popular culture,

> *…must countenance and make account for the way in which the meaning of any text is produced and negotiated across a plethora of websites, social media, press releases and discussion fora. It's therefore important to acknowledge and make reference to the array of paratextual materials that will inform the analysis. (p. 19)*

The paratextual is a key feature in the representations of effeminacy and bottom identities explored in this book. Not only does it emphasise the challenge of containing specific texts, the paratextual also underlines the way in which readers and viewers also personally identify themselves with a given work, especially sexually explicit material. Furthermore, the paratextual demands a methodological response that acknowledges the serendipitous ways in which online porn is browsed and through which users experience a sense of flow and arousal that cannot be 'captured' or 'contained' through rigid sampling techniques (Arroyo, 2016; Williams, 2003). In a sense, then, my book is engaging with material in ways that are especially inviting of a 'risk-filled interpenetration of the knower and the known', as Palmer writes (see also Chapter 3). It fully acknowledges this as a methodological consideration that also impacts the so-called 'content' to be analysed.

STRUCTURE OF THE BOOK

The book is divided into two halves. Part One: Theories, Perspectives and Sources explores the nature of gender nonconformity among same-sex attracted males from sociocultural, historical, and psychobiological perspectives, while also interrogating the variety of bottom identities that exist, from *faggy bottom* to *power bottom* (Chapter 1). This half of the book also examines the importance of marginalisation and belonging in relation to gender nonconforming experience and bottom identities. It highlights key places and spaces across the lifespan in which effeminacy and bottom identities grow, intersect and relate to each other – including in utero, in the family/home, school, LGBTQ+/gay 'community' and online (Chapter 2). The section ends by considering the diversity of creative narratives to be explored in Part Two, and why together they represent an important corpus exploring personal experiences of effeminacy and bottom identities (Chapter 3).

Part Two: Readings, Concerns and Directions begins by exploring the politics and challenges negotiated by males in the narratives under discussion, who experience effeminacy, bottoming and same-sex desire simultaneously, and asks whether it's possible, in today's climate, to be all three in a positive, self-affirming way (Chapter 4). It then explores fem bottoms in practice, focusing especially on how erotic models and online gay porn and erotica navigate the desires and identities of effeminate gay bottoms (Chapter 5). The final chapter in this section explores the connection between effeminate belonging and sexual wellbeing, by considering how the places and spaces explored in this book might shape and influence the sexual wellbeing of gender nonconforming bottoms in Western and global majority settings (Chapter 6).

The book can be read in a number of ways. Those interested in an interdisciplinary overview of effeminacy, gender nonconformity and gay bottom identities will find Chapter 1 particularly useful. Those interested in how effeminacy and bottom identities have implications for belonging and marginalisation will benefit especially from Chapter 2. For readers more drawn to an exploration of these concerns in film, media, porn and documentary, Chapters 4 and 5 will be particularly relevant. And for readers interested in the implications of effeminacy, bottom identities and belonging for wellbeing, Chapter 6 will be helpful.

NOTES

1. Ethel Person and Lionel Ovesey also distinguish between types of queen, with one being a 'passive, effeminate homosexual' and another being a 'drag "queen"', the latter of which may also take an insertive role in anal sex with masculine partners, whereas the former is usually receptive. These authors are also fairly critical of effeminate homosexuals/queens, with much talk of 'psychopathology' and 'disorder': these scholars rarely consider effeminacy in a positive light.
2. As I will demonstrate, *queen* is not synonymous with *drag queen*, lately popularised by *RuPaul's Drag Race*. While most drag queens are queens, only a few queens are drag queens.
3. See also Carrillo (2002, pp. 31–33) for a discussion of what it means to have a sexual identity. Carrillo, drawing on Epstein (1987), notes that the term 'sexual identity' began to appear in social scientific literature in the 1950s but became more standard in sociological analysis in the 1970s.

NOTES ON TERMINOLOGY

The Anglo-American analytical distinction between sex, gender and sexuality (or sexual orientation) has been contested beyond the Western context, and as this book shows, non-Western labels for effeminate bottoms – often used as 'street language' – regularly conflate all three and look for symmetries and asymmetries between them (Murray, 1996, p. 165). In this book, *sex* refers specifically to genetic sex as male or female; *gender* refers, here at least, to the growth, development and presentation of mixes of *masculinity*, *femininity* and *effeminacy*, which may be socially or culturally conditioned, but nevertheless arises or is built around individual constitutions that are embodied (see Chapter 2).[1] *Sexuality* refers to the growth, development and presentation of sexual desire towards others (and/or towards oneself). *Effeminate Belonging* explores how bottoms attempt to negotiate these different facets of themselves and understand the relationships between them, with implications for marginalisation and belonging.

With difficulty, therefore, the use of the terms *male* and *men* in this book, especially in relation to effeminate bottoms, is descriptive of their phenotypical sex and generally has little bearing on their sense of gender expression. As I will show, in some non-Western cultures, effeminate bottoms are excluded, and willingly exclude themselves, from the category of men: they are 'not-men', as Don Kulick has called them (1998; Stief, 2017). Even the queens of 20th-century Britain distinguished themselves from the men they sought as sexual partners; the queens were male, but not necessarily perceived as *men* (Baker, 2020; Houlbrook, 2005).

However, it's also the case that even in cultures containing 'not-men', effeminate bottoms are often considered a type of man and not usually a kind of woman or third, intermediary sex, even though they are gender nonconforming (Murray, 1995, p. 12). Fernández-Alemany and Murray have said of Honduran society:

> *At the level of natal/biological sex, there is a consensus that homosexuals [effeminate bottoms] are males, not women trapped*

---

[1] I discuss the terms *effeminacy* and *gender nonconforming* in detail in Chapter 1.

> *in male bodies or a third sex. It is in this sense of biological sex that these* hombres *refer to homosexuals of incomplete masculinity as* 'hombres'. *(2002, p. 112)*

The same kind of consensus is at work in contemporary online media discourses of the *boiwife* and *pussyboy*: they are males who on one level are men, but on another level are not men, depending on the context (see Chapter 5).

I aim to try to respect these contextual nuances, noting that some fem bottoms shy away from claiming affinity with the typical man of their culture while also recognising that they are still part of the male sex and may, in certain contexts, consider themselves and be considered by others as men and able to access certain male privileges associated with their culture. This approach also has implications for the wider theme of belonging, as Chapter 2 explores, with regard to the often-fraught connection between appearing as a man, but feeling disconnected from this and identifying more with women in one's culture – a phenomenon also shared by some heterosexual males, of course.

It's for this reason that this book does not explicitly discuss trans identities in any great depth. Nearly all the narratives exploring effeminacy and bottom identities I discuss position these two facets as an experience associated with cisgender males who identify as male, albeit with some shying away from calling themselves men, unless used only to describe their phenotypical sex. Part of the rationale for conceptualising effeminate belonging is that, for some males at least, effeminacy decidedly belongs as a phenomenon within the cisgender male experience: such males are gender nonconforming but also paradoxically sex normative (see also Thomas, 2017, for a discussion of trans in relation to 'sissy' identities). In the future, however, attention to trans bottom identities and practice is needed to give a more comprehensive picture of the contemporary 'bottom landscape'.

Meanwhile, I refer to *LGBTQ+*, *LGBTQ+ community* and *LGBTQ+-identified people* as pertaining to membership or identification with a recognisably Western construct rather than a self-evident sexual or gender identity that can easily be applied to non-Western settings. Finally, my use of the term 'passive' (i.e. 'sexually passive') to refer to males who bottom or identify as a bottom is not intended to capitulate to normative notions of bottoms who always 'bend over and take it' and are barely responsive. I use the term, without repetitive quotation marks, to denote historical or cross-cultural labels while also recognising that Romance language translations of *bottom* are linguistically closer to *passive* than they are to *bottom*.

NOTES ON RESEARCH ETHICS

Not only does this book explore sexually explicit narratives which require sensitive, respectful and attentive reading, but many of them are also created and circulated through social media and online forums. As media scholars have noted, such content can represent an ethical grey area for researchers: should content be attributed to those who produce it? How does a researcher utilise material when the original creators of that content may be unaware that researchers are interested in it?

The fact that such material exists in the public domain is not in itself a sufficient reason to follow ordinary scholarly attribution habits, such as citing quotations against an author's published (user)name. For example, Chapter 5 explores sexual writing and imagery published on social media sites such as Tumblr and Reddit, as well as viewer comments on porn sharing websites. Some of these comments are also controversial in that they cast slurs or criticisms against porn actors on the basis of perceived effeminacy or feminised traits. However, other social media content explored in this book is neither intended to be pornographic nor derogatory, demanding a somewhat modified approach to citation. In light of this, I have made the following decisions about attribution.

Following guidelines by media scholars Fiesler and Proferes, I have chosen to anonymise identifying information when quoting from pornographic social media posts and viewer comments on porn sharing sites (2018, p. 10). This decision is particularly salient in relation to those users who post derogatory comments about porn actors (Brody et al., 2022, p. 4). While I feel it's important and useful to analyse these comments in their original vocabulary and their importance for representing gendered and sexual practices and identities, I am also mindful of not wishing to draw attention to or cause harm to those who are responding to erotic material under a deliberately anonymous guise. I will therefore also not be including URL links to such online content and, where necessary, will also paraphrase or modify posts to avoid them being traced via internet searches (Greenhalgh et al., 2021).

However, I will include URL links to social media posts that are neither pornographic nor derogatory about others, such as those about bottom shaming or stigma associated with being a bottom and/or with being effeminate. This is partly in recognition that these internet posts may still be of use to my readers who want to learn about how LGBTQ+ individuals are conceptualising sexual practices online, thereby following the suggestion by Fiesler and Proferes that 'publication of user identity should only occur when the benefits of doing so clearly outweigh the potential harms' (2018, p. 10). I will also include URL links and author names for erotic stories published online, given the genre difference and expectation that fictional stories have an author and that author names can be legitimately pseudonymised.

Finally, I am driven by two overarching considerations. The first is to be as ethically sensitive as possible when handling sexual material, especially by those who circulate and produce such material under online personas and an expectation of anonymity. But I am also mindful of how these users form counterpublics online by producing and sharing sexually explicit material (Warner, 2002), or what Cavalcante describes as a 'public that caters to the marginalised and disenfranchised' (Cavalcante, 2017, p. 117). In a book which not only explores different modes of belonging among gender nonconforming males and/or bottoms, but also seeks to use the book as an opportunity to galvanise such belonging for marginalised people, the question of privacy and community is especially potent. I have aimed for an overall contextual approach, considering the specific contexts in which online speech utterances occur, the uses to which they have and might be put, while also considering the inadvertent consequences for counterpublic formation if solicitude for privacy is taken to unnecessary extremes.

Part 1

THEORIES, PERSPECTIVES AND SOURCES

1

GENDER NONCONFORMITY, EFFEMINACY AND GAY BOTTOM IDENTITIES

This chapter is divided into two sections that explore the relationship between gender nonconformity, effeminacy and gay bottom identities in the academic literature as well as online LGBTQ+ media. It explores effeminacy and gay bottom identities among gay males from sociocultural, historical, and psychobiological angles and questions the current separation of sexual orientation from gender expression and sex role when studying gay men. This chapter therefore sets out the key concepts and debates.

1.1 DEEP STRUCTURES? GENDER NONCONFORMITY, EFFEMINACY AND BOTTOM ROLES/IDENTITIES

Defining gender nonconformity in today's LGBTQ+ climate is not easy. The LGBTQ Centre at Montclaire State University, for example, defines someone who is gender nonconforming as 'a person who [...] either by nature or by choice does not conform to gender-based expectations of society (ex. Transgender, transsexual, intersex, genderqueer, cross-dresser, etc.)' (Montclaire State University, n.d.). This definition is not exactly helpful, however, because it simply directs a reader to other labels that also have definitions. *Genderqueer*, for instance, is described as 'a gender variant person whose gender identity is neither male nor female, is between or beyond genders, or is some combination of genders. Individuals that identify as genderqueer often challenge gender stereotypes and the gender binary system' (Montclaire State University, n.d.). It's not entirely clear, then, how a genderqueer person differs from a gender-nonconforming one, or indeed how both can be distinguished from a gender variant individual, or, still, from anyone who 'challenges gender stereotypes' – an extremely broad remit that may, by some definitions, encompass many men and women in post-industrial Western societies. Crucially, none of these definitions have anything to say about such a person's sexuality.

By contrast, *effeminacy* is a term that can be more easily pinned down. Unlike *gender nonconforming*, effeminacy has always been associated nearly exclusively with males and for most of the 20th century has also had sexual connotations. Merriam-Webster, for example, defines *effeminate* in the adjective form as 'having feminine qualities untypical of a man'. In 1975, US researchers even attempted to offer a quantitative rating scale to measure effeminacy in adult men as opposed to boys.[1] They sought to move beyond 'pejorative' terms such as *swishy*, *faggy* and *flaming queens* and offer something indicating the actual 'behavioral properties involved' (Schatzberg et al., 1975, p. 32). 67 items were proposed, framed as questions and divided into categories of speech, gait, posture and tonus, mouth movements, upper face and eyes, hand gestures, hand and torso gestures, body type, body narcissism and other – 'Does he take his shoes off during the interview?' (!). My personal favourite is: 'As he walks, do his buttocks noticeably roll in an up-and-down direction?' (p. 34).

There are of course a host of difficulties associated with a scale like this, not least its behavioural reductionism and risks associated with medicalising effeminacy and therefore suggesting it is pathological – something to be remedied rather than accepted and destigmatised. But as a historical document, the Effeminacy Scale offers a glimpse into attempts to define what effeminacy means. It is also instructive for thinking of effeminacy beyond *stereotypical* effeminacy: the flamboyant and the camp, often associated with cross-dressing.

Sex researchers investigating gender nonconformity have usually also seen effeminacy as something deeper or more pervasive (see below and Chapter 2): a sensitive, quiet, 'soft' gay man interested in 'feminine' pursuits and rejecting 'masculine' ones but who mostly dresses in recognisably male clothing can be read as effeminate or gender nonconforming just as more flamboyant effeminate gay men can. C. A. Tripp's division of effeminacy into *nelly*, *swish*, *blasé* and *camp* was also an attempt in the 1970s to emphasise the diversity of American effeminacy, with *nelly* being the least flamboyant variety: 'It is notably lacking in hostility, in bitchy qualities, or any flamboyance', wrote Tripp, 'and consequently has the remarkable characteristic of being obvious without being loud. Nelly males tend to be unusually gentle; they seem never to be intrusive or sharp-tongued' (1977, p. 178).

Tripp's typology underscores the fact that *effeminacy* and *femininity*, when it comes to males, are not always interchangeable. As scholars have pointed out, when we talk about a gay male being 'fem', 'nelly' or 'queeny', the traits that indicate such a description rarely find direct correspondence in females. Gay voice, a swishy walk, elegant posture, sartorial aesthetics and even talk of 'fem energy' indicate femininity *refracted through maleness*. As Rictor Norton has pointed out, quoting Judy Grahn, there is a 'gay cultural tradition' in which effeminacy in males is distinguished from femininity in females: 'the sweet sibilant faggot speech is peculiar to gay men, and completely distinctive' (2016, p. 20).

As I discuss in Chapter 5, it's also the case that for men who are attracted to fem bottoms – and they do exist – part of their attraction or sex object choice is rooted in the bottom's maleness, even if such bottoms are perceived to be effeminate. These men are attracted to aspects of femininity refracted through a recognisably male presentation; when such a male is able to 'pass' as a female, the attraction typically ceases. Hence the contemporary difference between twink bottoms and other femboy identities: the twink bottom has a recognisably male presentation, despite being often seen as effeminate, whereas other fem identities may branch more extensively into female presentation.

However, I am aware that not everyone – including gay men themselves – like the words *effeminacy* and *effeminate*, and it's for this reason that *fem* is often used precisely to indicate something that isn't the same as *feminine* but carries less historical baggage than *effeminacy*. But due to the way in which gay-identified online users and media commentators still regularly use the words *effeminate* and *fem* interchangeably, I will maintain this usage. But I fully recognise that for some readers, *effeminate* still carries negative and even medicalised connotations that are distasteful to them. I hope, however, that by emphasising the cultural and historical dimensions of effeminacy, as well as interrogating psychobiological discourses surrounding it, a middle path can be taken. But what about a longer historical treatment of *effeminacy*?

While scholars studying the classical world have routinely argued that effeminacy need not signify same-sex attraction or behaviour – 'a soft, romantic disposition in men could be taken as a sign of effeminacy' – let alone identification with sexual 'passivity', scholarly consensus on the nature of effeminacy in early modern Europe to the present is equally contested (Hennen, 2001, 2008; Williams, 2010, p. 158). Indeed, Peter Hennen has preferred to speak of 'effeminacies', plural, rather than a singular cultural or historical expression of effeminacy (Hennen, 2001).

In his history of King James I of England and his homosexuality, Michael Young notes the tendency among historians to minimise the role of effeminacy in the history of male homosexuality. 'It is frequently asserted', Young writes, 'that pre-modern constructions of homosexuality were not yet linked to effeminacy' (2021, p. 17). He goes on to show that effeminacy, defined similarly to the definition provided by Merriam-Webster, 'was an integral part of Jacobean discourse about sexual relations between males', thus predating even Randolph Trumbach's pinpointing of the marriage of effeminacy and homosexuality to the 18th century (Trumbach, 1998; Young, 2021, p. 18).

The historian Rictor Norton has likewise argued persuasively that it's simply not true to say, as scholars such as Alan Sinfield and David Halperin have done, building on Foucault, that (1) before the late 19th century there were only homosexual acts rather than homosexual, same-sex attracted persons, and (2) that effeminacy only became linked to homosexuality after the trial of Oscar Wilde, in 1895 (Halperin, 1990; Norton, 2016; Sinfield, 1994). The latter assertion still echoes in contemporary LGBTQ+ media, as a 2020 article on Vice.com demonstrates, arguing that the genealogy of the effeminate bottom stereotype can be linked to Oscar Wilde (Greig, 2020).

Stephen Murray has shown in his brilliant study of male homosexuality across cultures that the effeminate, sexually passive male-attracted male has in fact been of cultural significance since classical times (Murray, 2000). Both top and bottom same-sex attracted males have, for a long time – certainly from before the trial of Oscar Wilde – been thought of as certain kinds of persons, with dispositions, bents and even orientations that marked them out – even if only as ideal types – as deviant, liminal or queer personalities, not simply as men who committed deviant acts (Murray, 1989; Norton, 2010).

The early modern sodomite, at least until the early 18th century, was primarily seen as a sexual insertor, whose counterpart was the receptive *catamite*, *ganymede*, *ingle* or *pathic* (Murray, 1989, p. 462). These terms indicate 17th-century cultural awareness of specific types that synergised same-sex attraction (oriented from males to males), specific penetrative sex roles (insertor/insertee) and possible gendered connotations. Norton has argued, for instance, that the sexually passive catamite was perceived as effeminate across several Romance languages in the early modern period (Norton, 2016, p. 105).

The history of effeminacy and homosexuality in the 20th century in Britain and North America is somewhat easier to argue for because it postdates the Wilde trial of 1895. George Chauncey's *Gay New York: Gender, Urban*

Culture, and the Making of the Gay Male World, 1890–1940 (1994) argues convincingly for the way in which *fairies* and *queers* – two of the main homosexual types in New York before the Second World War – thought of themselves, were thought of by others, and were distinguished from *roughs* or *trade*, with whom fairies and queers had sex and sometimes built long-term relationships with in a form of heterogender homosexuality. The fairy (or alternatively the *pansy* or *queen*) was conceived of as an effeminate, passive male homosexual who was attracted to masculine 'normal' men.

With varying degrees of flamboyancy, the fairy can be read as a 20th-century manifestation of a type of gender nonconforming, sexually receptive male attracted to masculine men that finds correlates in other time periods and in different places. In Britain, a very similar parallel was found at the same time between *queans* and men (Houlbrook, 2005). According to Murray's typology of homosexualities, which consists of age-stratified, gender-stratified (or heterogender), and egalitarian types, the fairy and the quean would be placed under gender-stratified or heterogender homosexuality, which also links the 18th-century English *molly* to the 20th-century Latin American *maricon*, 'with expectations of feminine gender presentation and of insertee sexual behavior' (Murray, 1989, p. 469).

Attempts to recognise and honour continuity over contingency, and hence to locate similar transhistorical and transcultural types of effeminate bottoms, is a methodological commitment that distinguishes key approaches to the study of gender and sexuality in the humanities and social sciences, between social constructionists on the one hand, and essentialists on the other – the latter often a term of derision employed by the former (Dynes, 1995; Norton, 2010). This is a long-standing and often bitter debate that need not be rehearsed in full here (see Halwani, 1998; LeVay, 1996), suffice to say that there are important reasons for nuancing social constructionist approaches, which dominate cultural studies and the wider humanities and social sciences. One needs to ensure that 'the psychophysiological *trait* sexual orientation [be] distinguished from the *expression* of that trait in terms of behavior, the *identities* assigned to those possessing that trait by the self and others, and the *meanings* associated with the trait in a particular culture' (Stief, 2017, pp. 73–74, original emphasis). This book therefore explores how 'personal homosexual identity arises in the first instance from within the individual, [and] may then be consolidated along lines suggested by the wider homosexual subculture as well as warped by the wider homophobic society' (Norton, 2010, p. 10).

Effeminate Belonging is thus interested in 'deep structures' of gender nonconformity, sexual receptivity and male attraction to men, sometimes called *androphilia*, and how these intersect to shape patterns of belonging and marginalisation among such males. Delineating deep structures enables one to 'transcend differences related to how male same-sex sexual attraction is socially constructed within culturally specific contexts' (Vasey & VanderLaan, 2014, p. 138). Crucially, it seems that scholars are finding it easier to delineate a deep structure of male androphilia when it's confined to sexually receptive males who are somewhat effeminate (Cardoso, 2005, 2007, 2012). In 1992, James Weinrich and colleagues proposed that 'there is a different kind of homosexuality – a personality type or a fairly discrete developmental path – in which childhood gender role was relatively feminine and in which receptive anal intercourse has become a highly preferred adult genitoerotic role' (1992, p. 583). Moreover, this is, they argued, a hypothesis that 'has substantial cross-cultural validation' (1992, p. 583).

More recent contributions have sought to link cross-cultural research into homosexual effeminacy to psychobiological research emphasising links between gender expression – as relatively gender nonconforming – and preferred anal sex role as a bottom (Stief, 2017; Tasos, 2022; VanderLaan et al., 2022). As Matthew Stief summarises, the major theory informing this work is the prenatal hormone theory of sexual orientation,

> ...which proposes that heterosexual attraction is part of a sex-typical psychophysiological and behavioral phenotype. Sex-atypical non-heterosexual attractions are hypothesized to result from variation in androgen levels during a critical period of fetal neurodevelopment when the basis for these adult sex differences is being established. (2017, p. 74; Arnold, 2009; Bao & Swaab, 2011; LeVay, 2017)

As Simon LeVay has pointed out in his book, *Gay, Straight, and the Reason Why: The Science of Sexual Orientation* (2017), the prenatal hormone theory of sexual orientation also posits that sex-atypical sexual attraction (such as being homosexual) may in some instances also be accompanied by gender-nonconforming traits involving voice, mannerisms, digit ratio (relative finger lengths), hobbies and interests, and, as boys, disinclination for rough-and-tumble play (Bao & Swaab, 2011; Lippa, 2020).

The prenatal hormone theory can be traced back to 1976 and is predicated on finding links between mammals and humans; in its current form, it also recognises the importance of different stages of androgen surges prenatally as well as perinatally and is focused on organisational effects of these androgens (or lack thereof) on the brain (Tasos, 2022). However, research using this theory is still often beset by the methodological failure to distinguish *between* gay men as well as between gay men and non-gay men, which is why it is often inconclusive (VanderLaan et al., 2022).

Psychologist Ashlyn Swift-Gallant and her colleagues have attempted to nuance the suggestion that gender-nonconformity and other sex-atypical traits are part of a 'package' of a sex-atypical shift in the womb that also includes homosexuality, by effectively returning to Weinrich's earlier hypothesis that this 'shift' was particularly pronounced in a subtype of bottom – those for whom bottoming and being a bottom have 'become a highly preferred adult genitoerotic role' and who are likely to have a bottom identity (Swift-Gallant et al., 2017, 2019; Weinrich et al., 1992, p. 583). As Weinrich argued, 'there is now and always has been something "special" about RAI [Receptive Anal Intercourse] which makes it predictable – that is, which allows researchers to correlate it with other aspects of personality' (Moskowitz, 2022; Weinrich et al., 1992, p. 584). Or, as Simon LeVay writes in *The Sexual Brain* (1994), such bottoms form a particular subgroup of gay men, 'for whom their preferred erotic role is in a sense a continuation of a life-long sex atypical form of self-expression' (p. 115).

The fact that research from multiple disciplinary perspectives seems to point to a deep structure of gender-nonconforming bottoms that finds clear correlates in differing cultures and time periods has important implications for the wider themes of belonging and marginalisation with which this book is concerned. What might it mean to belong to a type that has historical and cross-cultural precedent? How might studying representations of marginalisation, stigma and shame associated with being an effeminate bottom mobilise a sense of shared affect and care among such bottoms? Is it possible to treat knowledge about psychobiological influences possibly shaping an effeminate bottom personality in ways that do not oppress the bottoms in question? And how might the attempt to triangulate available cross-disciplinary evidence exploring gender nonconformity and anal sex role preferences transform the broader study of gender and sexuality stemming from a humanities and social science impulse? These are questions the book seeks to engage with.

1.2 GENDER EXPRESSION, SEX ROLE AND SEX OBJECT CHOICE: BOTTOMS THE WORLD OVER

If the academic research on gender nonconformity and being a bottom continues to emphasise possible links between the two phenomena, why does LGBTQ+ media typically not do the same? This section explores how

Anglo-American LGBTQ+ media writes about bottoms and bottoming, highlighting the broader political insistence on separating sexual orientation from gender expression and anal sex role preference and behaviour. It questions whether, in the case of effeminate bottoms, this separation is helpful, by turning to Freud's distinction between sexual aim and sexual object, and by indicating some of the key challenges facing any cross-cultural analysis of bottom identities with a focus on effeminate ones.

By focusing on the diversity of ways in which media communicates issues of gender and bottoming, this section also emphasises the importance of leaning into a multiplicity of knowledge producers when exploring these topics. Media representations and discussions, which often utilise creative or artistic methods, help shape LGBTQ+ identities and perspectives as much as, if not more than, strictly 'academic' voices (Cavalcante, 2017; Plummer, 1995; Wignall, 2022).

1.2.1 From Faggy Bottom to Power Bottom: A Multiplicity of Bottoms?

In a 2022 article for Pink News, Josh Milton aims to subvert the dominant understanding of bottoms as somehow effeminate. He writes – partly in jest – that bottoms and bottoming have a 'surprisingly versatile history'. The article focuses on the historical power dynamics associated with being the penetrated male, highlighting the importance of the 'power bottom' as a way to subvert stereotypes of the effeminate, submissive bottom (see also Allan, 2016). Writing for Vice.com, James Greig questions whether there even is a bottom 'identity': 'This idea of "bottom" as being a fully-fledged identity category is, for the most, part tongue in cheek – which is why it's so fun swapping the word "women" for "bottom" in famous phrases' (2020). Taking a step further, Alex Green has argued that 'bottoming or topping is not a subjectivity; it's a thing you *do*. Once it's over, it's over – literally' (2020, original emphasis).

Assuming, as I do, that there can be a subjectivity or identity associated with bottoming, meaning that bottoming is something which impacts a sense of self-awareness as a specific kind of person – a position Greig eventually reaches – how does Anglo-American LGBTQ+ media represent the range of bottom identities or subjectivities out there? This can be divided into two main types that are often pitted against each other: the *fem* or *faggy bottom* and the *power bottom*, who is usually coded as masculine. These identities are often also positioned by LGBTQ+ media on a historical timeline, echoing Chauncey's delineation of the 'butch shift' from *fairy* to *clone*, effeminate to masculine, except that this shift in bottom identities can be pinpointed more specifically to the HIV-AIDS crisis and the rejection of effeminate connotations of bottoming (Chauncey, 1994; Milton, 2022).

The conventional Western bottom identity is largely feminised, and often – though by no means always – associated with the body type of the *twink* – a young(-looking), slender, relatively hairless gay male (Brennan, 2016a; Mercer, 2017). In the 1940s, he may have been called a *pansy* – 'notable for a slight body', although the pansy, as with the *queen*, was not age-bound in the way the twink is (Stines, 2017, p. 131). As Brian O'Flynn argues for i-D Magazine, the twink may be quintessentially gay rather than straight and is often read as a proxy for an effeminate bottom, but at its core, a twink is first and foremost a male body type.

Gay porn scholar Joseph Brennan has explored how the *twink* as a contemporary term for an effeminate bottom has captured the wider gay imagination (on the internet forum, Data Lounge), in relation to British diver, Tom Daley. Brennan argues that Daley's ostensibly gender-nonconforming presentation, combined with his body type, leads some to conclude automatically that he is a bottom (2016b). As one blogger has put it in relation to Daley's effeminate 'gay face': '"pussy" has never sprung to anyone's mind when they thought about Tom Daley. Unless it was preceded by "boy"'. However, as Daley has gotten older and become a parent himself, it's interesting to witness how some Data Lounge commentators are using the word *queen* in reference to him, to fantasise about his effeminate bottomhood extending beyond his 'twink years'.

In a sense, this coupling of *twink* and *queen* to denote an effeminate bottom at different stages in life also has precedent in classical Rome; the poet Martial, for example, linked Ganymede (the prototypical *catamite*) to the *cinaedus* (from the Greek *kinaidos*) – an effeminate male presumed to be sexually passive – suggesting that if a *catamitus* does not desist from his effeminate bottomhood as an adult male, he will become a *cinaedus* (Williams, 2010, p. 206). Similarly, if a twink does not man up, he is at risk of becoming a queen, in the general sense of being an effeminate bottom.

The effeminate twink bottom, however, is only one contemporary type among a constellation of other contemporary fem bottom types, including the *nelly bottom, bottom faggot, pussyboy,* and *boiwife,* and the generic submissive bottom, all of which avoid placing an age fence and body type around such an individual in the way *twink* does (Vytniorgu, 2024b). But it should be emphasised that there is no one word that encapsulates *fem gay bottom* in the same way as the non-Western identities discussed below and the historical Western identities described above.

As a label, *bottom* is often coupled with adjectives to denote greater specificity. American linguist Arnold Zwicky has reclaimed the adjective *faggy* to describe these gender-nonconforming bottom types, to encapsulate the central place of gender expression in shaping how specific bottoms present and think of themselves. Through his blog (https://arnoldzwicky.org), much of which is dedicated to themes of gender and sexuality and gay porn, Zwicky has developed a sophisticated discourse of bottom identities and subjectivities, ranging from *faggy bottom* to *butch fagginess* – a hybrid 'homomasculine' blend of traditional fagginess or effeminacy and traditional masculinity that typically resides in more muscular, hirsute and 'butch' men (Duggan, 2002; Zwicky, 2018). The way in which Zwicky has communicated a range of identity labels and experiences to represent a blend between masculine and effeminate gay subjectivity is also in part due to the medium of his blog, which invites readers to engage with his content and explore it in non-linear ways through concentrating on tags or keywords which operate through hyperlinks. Thus, Zwicky can present what seems to be well-theorised concepts with copious illustrative material in a relatively short space of time (within a few years).

In a 2019 post, Zwicky writes about a man called Todd (pseudonym):

> *Todd saw himself as a gay/queer man (that is, as a man and as a man whose sexual desires were directed at other men), but as a particular species or subtype of queer, namely a sissy, a homomasculine identity that for him meant not actual identification with women, but instead an identification with a particular ideal of fagginess.* (2019)

Zwicky's concept of butch fagginess departs from discourses of the fem submissive bottom to demonstrate how for some bottoms, masculinity and femininity can blend in a way that only makes sense by referring to it as *butch fagginess* – something distinctly male and confident, but not conventionally masculine. As I note above, *effeminacy* and *femininity* are distinct enough to warrant separate analysis, and *fem gay bottom* is probably more accurately shorthand for *effeminate gay bottom* rather than *feminine gay bottom*. Effeminacy, or 'butch fagginess' (which emphasises the maleness of effeminacy) is the presence of fem typical traits in males.

In the same post, Zwicky suggests that *genderqueer* might, under some circumstances, also be an appropriate term for what butch fagginess represents. However, Zwicky subsumes all of these forms of gender-nonconforming expression among gay men under the broad umbrella of 'f-gays', or what 'critics' might characterise as:

...effeminate, fem, femme, flamboyant, flaming, fag, faggy, faggot, fairy, fairy-boy, camp, campy, mincing, prissy, nelly, pansy, nancy, nancy-boy, swish, stereotypical, gay-acting, too gay. (2022)

So, although for Zwicky there may be variations in how effeminacy is expressed in gay men, the general effect is fairly similar, of being different and subversive of normative standards of masculinity while still being recognisably male.

In recent years the popularity of the power bottom has increased, as an alternative to the more restrictive category of submissive fem bottom encapsulated in the twink; although the concept of a *power bottom twink* also exists (Brennan, 2016a). Writing for the magazine Men's Health, Zachary Zane explains that 'there are a ton of stereotypes associated with bottoms, such as being more effeminate, submissive, and emotionally needy. Being a power bottom bucks those stereotypes and shows that bottoms can be dominant, commanding, and masculine, too' (2021). The role and/or identity of the power bottom seems to be a way for men who have sex with men to maintain a sense of their bottoming as an extension of their manhood, even reaching far beyond this, within a BDSM context, to practices of barebacking, being a faggot, and celebrating 'pig masculinities' that aim to move beyond an equivalence of effeminacy and bottom identity (Dean, 2009; Florêncio, 2020; Mercer, 2017; Underwood, 2003).

In a contemporary LGBTQ+ Western culture in which masculinity and even butch fagginess is deemed more desirable than *nellies*, *bottom queens* and *faggy bottoms*, the position of effeminacy is precarious (Sarson, 2020; Vytniorgu, 2023). It's not simply about endorsing effeminacy or gender nonconformity in gay males and other same-sex attracted males. It's about allowing the cultural space in which effeminacy and bottom identities can coalesce in ways that also avoid the lumping together of these as an act of prejudice directed at those for whom this combination is unsuitable.

One of the reasons why it's currently difficult to speak about the two together in Anglo-American LGBTQ+ media is that, while a masculine power bottom still synergises gender positionality and bottom identity (Hoppe, 2011), an effeminate bottom does so in ways that foreground the gender positionality in ways that are deemed unacceptable and politically suspect (Green, 2020). In other words, the effeminate bottom insists on the mutually reinforcing role, for them, of sex object choice (often masculine men), anal sex role preference (as a bottom), and gender expression (as unmasculine, effeminate and gender nonconforming). To understand this contested relationship, we need to return to Freud.

1.2.2 Was Freud Right?

In the first of his *Three Essays on the Theory of Sexuality* (1905), Freud made the distinction between sexual object and sexual aim, particularly while discussing the phenomenon of homosexuality and thereby framing himself as a sexologist in the manner of Karl Heinrich Ulrichs, Magnus Hirschfeld and Richard von Kraft-Ebbing. He writes: 'Let us call the person from whom sexual attraction proceeds the *sexual object* and the act towards which the instinct tends the *sexual aim*' (1975, p. 2). In other words, sexual object refers to the focus of a person's sexual attraction, or rather, the *orientation* of one's attraction – being same-sex attracted, or attracted to masculine men or effeminate bottoms, for example. Sexual aim refers to the behaviour and presentation of self which is designed to secure a response from those to whom we are sexually oriented – positioning oneself as masculine or effeminate, top or bottom, for example.

Freud then proceeds to frame these terms in the language of deviation: deviation of sexual object (an 'inverted' sexual orientation), and a deviation of sexual aim (for example, interest in receptive anal sex). As Chauncey has argued, the relevance of Freud's distinction between sexual object and sexual aim is that, unlike other sexologists such as Ulrichs or Hirschfeld, Freud (and Havelock Ellis as well) argued that these two aspects were essentially separated. Ulrichs had argued that, while it was possible to find otherwise typically masculine men who happened to be oriented towards other males – often effeminate ones, it was also common to find males whose sexuality and gender expression were fundamentally 'inverted' – who were effeminate, enjoyed passive anal intercourse, and who were attracted to masculine men. He termed these males *weiblings* – possibly a late-19th-century version of the 1780s *weichling*, coined by Joseph Jacob von Plenck (Janssen, 2017, p. 1852; LeVay, 1996, p. 14). Freud, on the other hand, argued for at least the conceptual separation of sexual object from sexual aim.

Chauncey has written persuasively about the way in which the middle-class in the mid-20th-century US grew to prioritise sexual object – or sexual orientation – over sexual aim, and to insist that one could be sexually attracted to other men and otherwise be just like other men:

> *The homosexual man, defined solely by his capacity to find sexual satisfaction with another male, began to emerge as a distinct figure in medical discourse, different from the invert, who was still defined by a more thoroughgoing inversion of gender conventions, and*

from the heterosexual man, who could find sexual satisfaction only with a female. (1994, p. 124)

While this is conceptually interesting, it should also be emphasised that at least until the 1940s in the United States and the United Kingdom, terms such as *homosexual* and *invert* only circulated within a small, middle-class scientific and intellectual community, and that on the working-class ground in New York and London, colloquialisms such as *fairy*, *poof* (or *pouf*), *quean/queen*, and *pansy* were noised abroad, immediately understood, and reflected an intuitive grasp of a form of non-normative self-awareness that linked together effeminacy, sexual orientation towards masculine 'normal' men and expectation of only sucking cock and/or being fucked, rendering the queen's penis functionally useless (see also Houlbrook, 2005, for a British analysis).

To answer my question, then, Freud was probably correct in separating sexual aim and sexual object – at least for analytical purposes – but what needs to be scrutinised is the way in which the latter has now come to dominate conversation around gay men. As we will see, sometimes this has been beneficial. By emphasising the primacy of sexual orientation, men who otherwise might have felt pressured to adopt gender-nonconforming behaviour and assume an exclusively passive sexual role, have been liberated to assimilate their sexual orientation as part of an otherwise fairly typical gender expression. They are just men who happen to be same-sex attracted.

On the other hand, there are difficulties for those who are gender-nonconforming gay bottoms and may even wish there was a language and space for them to belong with these three inter-related aspects of themselves. Turning to non-Western and global majority examples shows that the triumph of sexual object over sexual aim is not universal (yet), and this provides fem bottoms in the West with a contextual frame of reference with which to nurture a sense of belonging.

1.2.3 Non-Western Gender-Nonconforming Bottoms

Gender-nonconforming bottoms have been observed in many non-Western countries and global majority settings, including the *kothi* in India and Bangladesh (Alam & Marston, 2023; Gill, 2016; Stief, 2017), the *skesana* in South Africa (Msibi & Rudwick, 2015; Ntuli, 2009), the *bakla* in the Philippines (Garcia, 2009; Manalansan, 2003), the *ciota* in Poland (Janion, 2022), the *tetka* in Eastern and Southeastern Europe (Baer, 2005; Lambevski, 1999), the *paneleiro*, *bicha*, *viado* and *maricón* in Brazil (Cardoso, 2005;

Carrier, 1976), the *loca* in Honduras (Fernández-Alemany & Murray, 2002), the *kūnī* in Iran (Guitoo, 2021), the *lubunya* in Turkey (Bereket & Adam, 2006) and the *jota* in Mexico (Prieur, 1998). Murray calls them 'male receptacles for phallic discharges' (2000, p. 255).

Allowing for the nuances of cultural variation due to the specific societies and time periods in which they are especially visible, as well as varying degrees of gender nonconformity, these effeminate bottom types nevertheless show remarkable similarity in characteristics (Whitam, 1980): strong preference to be sexually receptive or passive; marked gender nonconformity in childhood and adulthood, including interest in 'women's work' and hobbies and dislike of typical male hobbies and occupations; a clear desire for men unlike themselves – manly, sexually insertive – and a similar dislike of sexual relations with other 'not-men' like themselves. As one Bangladeshi *kothi* said recently, 'I will not be attracted to any feminine man. I like a man who is masculine or manly' (Alam & Marston, 2023, p. 9). They are typically also located among the working classes and have less contact with Western-influenced LGBTQ+ lifestyles and politics. In other words, they sound like the pre-war *fairies* and *queens* of the United States and Britain.

As early as the 1970s, researchers were discovering the gendered connotations attached to males who assumed the passive role in anal sex with men in global majority contexts – particularly Latin American ones. In his study of Mexican male homosexuality, Joseph Carrier argued that in Mexico 'an equivalence is always made between the effeminate male and the homosexual male' (Carrier, 1976, p. 111). In his 1971 study of Mexican *maricones* (translated in English by Carrier as *sissy*, *fairy*, or *queer*), Carrier noted that a large proportion of 'anal passive males having adult homosexual contacts remembered themselves as being slightly to very effeminate children, whereas the anal active males having adult homosexual contacts did not' (Carrier, 1971, p. 290; Thing, 2009).

In India and Bangladesh, *kothi* is a term used 'by many effeminate men to signal their preference for being passive (bottom) partners during sexual intercourse among men who have sex with men (MSM)' (Gill, 2016, p. 1). In English, *kothi* can be translated as 'fag' or 'sissy' (Gill, 2016, p. 1). Fernando Cardoso's study of the *paneleiro* in Brazil highlights a similar system of heterogender homosexuality to that of the *kothi*, despite being culturally and geographically dissimilar to India (Cardoso, 2005). The *paneleiros* whom Cardoso interviewed mostly preferred receptive anal intercourse and enjoyed performing oral sex in comparison to the men interviewed who had sexual relations with *paneleiros*. Furthermore, in the same way as the Indian and Bangladeshi *kothis*, these Brazilian *paneleiros* refused to have sex with other *paneleiros*, 'since they prefer "real men"' (Alam & Marston, 2023; Cardoso, 2005, p. 105).

A complementary system of heterogender male homosexuality was highlighted by Annick Prieur in her study of Mexican *jotas*, who were described 'as effeminate men who are penetrated by other men' (Carrillo, 2002; Prieur, 1998, p. 10). *Jotas*, like the *kothis* and *paneleiros*, will rarely if ever seek sexual contact with each other. As in other places where heterogender homosexuality is popular, such effeminate bottoms seek a more masculine man. In Turkey, the effeminate passive *lubunya* typically rejects sexual contact with another *lubunya*: 'it is impossible for another feminine man to establish same-sex bonds with him, as two "women" would have nothing to offer to each other' (Bereket & Adam, 2006, p. 139).

Recently, Arash Guitoo has explored the Iranian *kūnī* in online sexual fantasy stories, and the *kūnī* (approximating the Western *faggot* or *poof*) approximates these other non-Western identities, while also adopting the Western 'gay' as an equivalent term for traditional heterogender understandings of same-sex subjectivity (2021, p. 890). Thabo Msibi and Stephanie Rudwick have outlined a similar model of identity and behaviour among African male IsiNgqumo speakers in South Africa, termed *skesana*, who adopt effeminate gender expression and a bottom sex role preference (2015). In contemporary Brazil, *poc* (or *pocpoc* – resembling the sound of heels clicking on the ground) is now used to describe effeminate or 'fruity' gays presumed to be bottoms (as opposed to 'people of colour'), along with older terms such as *bicha* (see also Chapter 4).[2]

Together, these studies and others like them highlight the long-standing, cross-cultural existence of gender-nonconforming homosexual bottoms in non-Western societies which position themselves within a heterogender sphere of male homosexuality. Under such a system, a male will only be perceived to be a homosexual or 'not-man' if they are effeminate (to varying degrees) and purported to be sexually passive in male anal sex (Fernández-Alemany & Murray, 2002; Garcia-Rabines, 2022; Kulick, 1998). Other pertinent commonalities include a preference for domestic tasks such as cooking, to emphasise one's gender nonconformity, and a strong preference for men who are starkly different from them in sexual object choice, sex role, and gender expression. The converse side of this latter preference is an aversion to sexual engagement with another fem bottom – what historically in 20th-century Britain was termed by Polari as *tootsie trade*, but which in many global majority settings is phrased around kneading dough or tofu, or, in Turkey, '*kapak kapağa vuruşturma*, literally meaning two lids/caps hitting each other' (Bereket & Adam, 2006, p. 139).

Each of these studies also notes the tensions at play between these traditional, often working-class expressions of effeminate bottom subjectivity, and the encroachment over time of the middle-class Western gay/LGBTQ+ egalitarian form of homosexuality, which has increased (but not entirely displaced traditional forms) since some of these studies were conducted (Garcia-Rabines, 2022), and which is now also along a generational divide, with older men sometimes adhering more strongly to traditional models (Thing, 2009). In India, Harjant Gill reports Western-identified gay men in Mumbai boycotting nightclubs if *kothis* were present, with a response from *kothis* and *hijras* to incorporate their identities into a LGBTKQH movement (Gill, 2016). In some countries heterogender male homosexuality now exists, to some degree, alongside egalitarian models, often in hybridised ways so that even the term *gay* has come to have local meanings that are not synonymous with 'American gay' (Gómez Jiménez et al., 2021; Vidal-Ortiz et al., 2009; see also Chapter 5).

What is pertinent for Western fem gay bottoms is that typically 'no one in societies in which gender-variant roles arise shares the Western analytical concern with specifying whether gender or sexuality is more important in defining these kinds of people' (Murray, 2000, p. 293). In other words, in their traditional conceptions of gender and sexuality, these non-Western settings refuse to make the Freudian separation of sexual object and sexual aim. While this might enable masculine insertors to fuck other males and leave their manhood largely intact, it means that effeminate 'not-men' who are fucked by 'normal men' hold a culturally recognisable if sometimes oppressed role. They might form long-lasting relationships with men, but they might also simply be 'a receptacle for phallic discharges' in cultures where extramarital sexual access to women is taboo (Guasch, 2011). As Murray makes clear, 'instrumental use, contempt, and violence (sexual and other) are the lot of effeminate men (cross dressed or not) in cultures influenced by the classic Mediterranean code of male honor' (2000, pp. 256–257).

Throughout the book, I will return to examples of global majority types of fem bottom to help contextualise Anglo-American negotiations of effeminacy, homosexuality and bottom identity and practice. In the next chapter, I discuss the complex experiences of marginalisation and belonging negotiated by gender-nonconforming bottoms.

NOTES

1. They were not in fact the first to do so. See also Chapter 12 of *Sex and Personality: Studies in Masculinity and Femininity* by Lewis Terman and Catherine Cox Miles (1936). Terman's connections to American eugenicist movements are now well-known. But Lowell Kelly's research for Chapters 11–13 is instructive for

attempts to quantify 'sexual inversion' in 'passive male homosexuals' during the time covered by George Chauncey's *Gay New York*, in which homosexual passive males were colloquially known as *queers* and *fairies*. Lowell notes however that the 'passive male homosexuals' he interviewed all referred to themselves as *queens* rather than *fairies*, with the majority preferring receptive anal sex over insertee oral sex, contrary to *fairies'* reported preference for insertee fellatio. For one of the first autobiographies of a self-identified *fairy*, see *Memoirs of an Androgyne* by Earl Lind [Ralph Werther] (1918).

2. For example, see https://revistamarieclaire.globo.com/Noticias/noticia/2018/08/poc-personagem-de-galisteu-explica-o-que-e-nova-giria-em-o-tempo.html (accessed 4 August 2023). In 2023, the music streaming service Spotify also released a playlist entitled 'pop poc' with an image of singer Troye Sivan on the cover (see also Chapter 4 for more on Sivan).

2

MARGINALISATION AND BELONGING

This chapter continues the conceptual mapping begun in Chapter 1 by turning to the concepts of marginalisation and belonging and how these might be experienced by gender-nonconforming bottoms. In the social sciences, there have been numerous studies around stigma and prejudice faced by effeminate gay males and bottoms (Brooks et al., 2017; Glick et al., 2007), but these studies tend to focus on adult experiences and overlook how different places and spaces might contribute to shaping experiences of feeling marginalised. This chapter considers some of these places and spaces in turn, after reflecting on the related concepts of marginalisation and belonging and how they might relate to gay men, and specifically fem bottoms. The chapter concludes by asking what it might mean to belong to an identity that has historical and cross-cultural evidence of being routinely stigmatised.

2.1 MARGINALISATION AND BELONGING

Sociologists have often described the prejudice faced by gay men in both Western and non-Western societies. In 1995, Ilan Meyer developed the term 'minority stress', originally coined by Virginia Brooks in 1981, this time to describe the various forms of difficulty faced by gay men in the United States because of their homosexuality, which included internalised homophobia, stigma and actual experiences of violence because of their sexual orientation (Brooks, 1981; Meyer, 1995). However, as others have argued since, it's also the case 'that for some the stigma of homosexuality is less concealable than for others. This may especially be true for homosexual people who are gender-atypical or gender-nonconforming' (Sandfort et al., 2007, p. 182). A 2005 study, for example, found that same-sex attracted young people with a history of gender nonconformity were more likely to report feeling different from their peers, even from other gay people who lacked a history of gender nonconformity (D'Augelli et al., 2005).

The important point here is that 'an effeminate gay man (EGM) violates norms of sexuality and personality, whereas a masculine gay man (MGM) violates norms of sexuality, but not of personality. As a result, attitudes are more negative toward the "doubly deviant" EGM than toward the MGM type' (Glick et al., 2007, p. 55; Worthen, 2024). A 2007 study found that 'when heterosexual people say they dislike gay men, a more accurate interpretation of this statement may be that they dislike *feminine gay men*' (Lehavot & Lambert, 2007, p. 288, original emphasis). Marginalisation of effeminate gay men has, sadly, even been noted among other gay men, such as in the 1950s US homophile movement, or in contemporary gay culture (Gerrard et al., 2023; Loftin, 2007; Taywaditep, 2002). Gay men who perceive (or wish to perceive) themselves as masculine 'may chronically distance themselves from feminine gay men', causing effeminate gay men to be the 'marginalised among the marginalised' (Hunt et al., 2016, p. 111; Taywaditep, 2002).

The situation is made even more complicated when sex role preference and behaviour are added to the mix. Being a bottom can cause social anxiety (Reilly et al., 2013), present challenges with identity formation (McGill & Collins, 2015), and elicit prejudice from others (Brooks et al., 2017). Negative feelings experienced by bottoms also seem to be transcultural and transhistorical, especially so in countries shaped by the Mediterranean outlook on gender and sexuality, which tends to make a natural equivalence between effeminacy and being sexually receptive, regardless of whether this is always accurate for specific individuals (Callahan & Loscocco, 2023; Murray, 2000; Nardi, 1998).

There might also be associations around bottoming with impurity and disease. In ancient Rome, *cinaedi* – effeminate males presumed to be sexually passive – were also thought to be impure and therefore to be avoided in polite social interaction; kissing a *cinaedus* was out of the question, given he was thought to be a cocksucker. Their depilated asses (a mark of a *cinaedus*) might also reveal what the poet Martial called 'swollen figs', or anal warts or haemorrhoids (Richlin, 1993, p. 551). During the AIDS crisis of the 1980s and 1990s, it was also strongly asserted that bottoms were more at risk of contracting the virus, and the figure of the unmasculine, emaciated 'passive homosexual' was thus linked with disease in the public imagination (Signorile, 1997). Effeminate bottoms seem to be perennially at risk of experiencing marginalisation, both from their heterosexual peers as well as from other gay men who may consider such males undesirable as sexual partners or as threats to the overall reputation of gay men's masculinity and even healthy sexuality (Ravenhill & de Visser, 2017, 2019).

One of the key points in an analysis of marginalisation faced by effeminate gay men and bottoms is that it's important to move beyond a simplistic attribution of marginalisation to homophobia. Instead, we should be talking more in terms of *effeminophobia* (Richardson, 2009; Sedgwick, 1991), *sissyphobia* (Bergling, 2001), or *femmephobia* (Hoskin, 2019), especially when these imply a stigma of being anally or orally penetrated as well. As I will show in my analysis of some of the narratives in the chapters that follow, sometimes this distinction between homophobia and effeminophobia is muddied to the extent that calls for social action are directed at countering homophobia as opposed to prejudice targeted specifically at gender nonconforming or effeminate boys and men who are presumed to be bottoms (or proto-bottoms). A term such as *effeminophobia*, originally coined by queer theorist Eve Kosofsky Sedgwick, specifically denotes a fear of gender nonconformity and effeminacy in males, which are often read as a proxy for being a gay bottom. Moreover, while Trevor Hoppe has argued that being a bottom might also be associated with more positive emotions such as pleasure and power, this seems to be the case mostly for non-effeminate bottoms and those who assume a 'power bottom' identity (2011).

What, then, might a sense of belonging entail for gay men, fem bottoms, and the wider LGBTQ+ community in the West? Recent research on LGBTQIA+ loneliness and belonging has suggested that a sense of belonging comes from being seen and accepted by other LGBTQ+ people (Jones & Vytniorgu, 2022). The ability to choose one's family and to feel part of a chosen kinship network is often very healing, especially if one has previous experiences of negative affect from parents, siblings, or wider family (Formby, 2017).

More broadly, belonging as a concept has gained in popularity since the early 2000s as a sociological and philosophical tool to explore affective dimensions of community, feeling included, and identification with cultures and identities which may also be historical and transcultural (Lähdesmäki et al., 2016; May & Muir, 2015). Vanessa May and Stewart Muir refer to belonging as an 'elusive concept' (2015, p. 2). But these authors also recognise that any exploration of people's sense of belonging needs to take into account multiple environments, 'such that we cannot talk of one, such as belonging to place, without necessarily talking about other aspects as well, such as belonging to a socio-cultural world' (p. 2). Belonging has also attracted criticism for the way in which it can be harnessed by extremist right-wing groups obsessed with exclusionary politics based on ethnic, religious and national identity, and often all three at the same time (see Rohr, 2019).

However, it remains unclear what a sense of belonging, in the positive and inclusive sense of the term, might mean specifically for fem bottoms. Most of the research to date has focused on understanding how marginalisation for gay bottoms occurs due to stigma and shame, not on how bottoms might articulate a sense of belonging. This book hopes to address this lack, but one of the ways to proceed is to think of marginalisation and belonging as being associated with different places and spaces in which these two interrelated experiences might occur over time, and to begin to envision it in this way.

Scholars across the humanities and social sciences have explored LGBTQ+ experiences through the so-called 'spatial turn' and geographies of sexualities, but a key area for further enquiry is understanding the impact of places and spaces – physical, online, and imaginary – on the consolidation of sexual identities over time, and the search for belonging through such identities (Bell & Valentine, 1995; Browne et al., 2009; Formby, 2017; Houlbrook, 2005). Moving towards a language of *effeminate belonging* means at the very least considering the significance of acceptance across a range of places and spaces; ease of articulation about one's sexual identity and experiences over time; and a sense of connection and affect towards others (and from others to oneself) in a range of spaces, not just among LGBTQ+-identified individuals.[1]

2.2 BELONGING IN DIFFERENT PLACES AND SPACES

2.2.1 Embodiment

Despite queer theory's scepticism of biological explanations of sexuality, there is evidence that what goes on prenatally and perinatally has a significant influence on humans' sexual orientation and gender expression. The 'sexual differentiation' of the brain takes place later than the sexual differentiation of the genitals (Savic et al., 2010). Organisation of the brain under sex hormones develops in the second half of pregnancy and can be divided into two main dimensions – knowledge which has been routinely accepted by scientists since its first articulation, in 1959 (Phoenix et al., 1959). The first aspect relates to what are called 'organisational effects', and the second aspect relates to what are termed 'activational effects'. The former is significant in influencing sexual orientation and a sense of one's gender as relatively conforming or non-conforming.

Androgens generally shift a male's brain in a male-typical way, which results in gendered behaviour that is observable within the first year of life (Bao & Swaab, 2011; Hines, 2011). As boys grow, patterns in play behaviour are also noticeable and can be explained in part by organisational differences that have shaped the brain in utero. As Melissa Hines notes:

> *Boys tend to prefer toys like vehicles, such as cars, trains, trucks and airplanes, and weapons, whereas girls tend to prefer toys like dolls and tea sets. Sex differences in toy preferences appear in infancy, at least by the age of 12 months, and they grow larger as children develop into middle childhood. (2011, p. 14)*

Attempts to engineer children's play behaviour or, still worse, to artificially counteract emerging gendered behaviour have routinely been found to fail, to say nothing of the ethics and the damage done to a child's sense of self (LeVay, 2017 and see below).

For gender-nonconforming or effeminate boys, the differences can be stark: they typically report not wanting to play like most of the boys around them and to prefer activities and toys more typical of those chosen by most (though by no means all) girls, hence why they are often labelled a *sissy, fag, poof, tapette, maricon, bakla* (etc.) by their peers (Bergling, 2001; Green, 1987; Pascoe, 2012). As they get older, they might also begin to display noticeably atypical male speech habits such as elongated vowels, vocal fry, sibilant /s/ and aspirated /t/ sounds, as well as other gender atypical body 'mannerisms', for which they feel they have no control over, but which are targeted as a proxy for a nascent homosexual orientation because they are read as unmasculine and distinctly effeminate (Johnson et al., 2007; Ravenhill & de Visser, 2017; Smyth et al., 2003; Suire et al., 2020). As one correspondent to the US homophile magazine *ONE* wrote in 1963, after being repeatedly called a 'blazing faggot', he began to,

> *…search the mirror carefully. At first I saw only what I had always seen. A young blond, five foot ten of slight build, sensitive face, and a neat appearance. Then I saw the gestures, the chiseled features, the dancer's grace, the tricky, sensitive smile. I DID blaze!*
>
> (quoted in Loftin, 2007, p. 589)

For this correspondent, who signed himself as John, attempts to alter his gender atypical expression were futile, and yet in a note of desperation, added: 'So reads the history of a blazing faggot who would give his right arm to be but a tiny spark' (p. 590).

Narratives of childhood gender nonconformity have repeatedly been identified by sex researchers investigating links between this and a later adult preference for same-sex desire, especially so for adult homosexual males with a strong preference for bottoming (LeVay, 2017; Swift-Gallant et al., 2021; Whitam, 1980; Zuger, 1988). Effeminate boys have often insisted on gender atypical preferences despite encouragement by parents and those in authority to socialise in more male-typical ways (Savic et al., 2010, p. 44). Sex researchers have therefore linked these sex differences and gender atypicalities to organisational influences – (epi)genetic, immunological, and endocrinological – on the brain, of which sexual orientation is just one manifestation.

What happens in utero and in the immediate weeks following birth (when, for boys, testosterone levels are especially high) is significant for contributing to early senses of belonging or feeling different from others. Persistently gender-nonconforming boys, whether or not they grow up to be same-sex attracted, are at risk of feeling somewhat marginalised and in search of a sense of belonging (Wallien & Cohen-Kettenis, 2008). Not only, as I discuss below, in spaces such as the home or school, but also in terms of embodied belonging and hence also belonging with their male peers at a time when children are often divided on the basis of their sexed bodies (for example, in spaces such as sports changing rooms).

Queer theorist Judith Butler has coined the term *liveable life* to suggest ways in which people's lives are made liveable through being recognised by others for whom they feel themselves to be (2004). Yet the problem for gender-nonconforming boys is that they *are* routinely recognised as being non-normative, yet this recognition does not translate into that life made liveable: they are still marginalised, and a sense of belonging is prevented. Rhetoric scholar Timothy Oleksiak has imagined how 'bottoming is carried in the body' through looks, gestures, and posture, but often these are precisely what result in such bottoms or suspected bottoms being treated in prejudicial ways, resulting in exclusion and marginalisation (2022, p. 358).

The fact that sexual differentiation of the genitals and reproductive system occurs earlier than the sexual differentiation of the brain means that firstly (Bao & Swaab, 2011), it's important to highlight – and normalise – the *range* of gendered behaviour possible among males and females, with effeminate males and 'butch' females being, in fact, sex 'normative' if also gender nonconforming (Kaiser et al., 2020), and that secondly, identifying more with the other sex, especially in childhood, may cause difficult emotions and a sense of non-belonging in the space of one's body (Bailey & Zucker, 1995; Li et al., 2017). As Tait Sanders and colleagues have noted of trans people, but which in this instance may also apply to gender-nonconforming boys, 'the collective effect of lived experiences of unrecognizability may result in feeling isolated or not belonging or feeling at home both within one's skin, and broader gendered society' (2023, p. 4). Moreover, an increasing self-awareness of behavioural differences such as the gay voice, mannerisms, and movement, however subjectively perceived and stereotypically understood, combine to underscore a sense of separation from one's peers, which can be extremely uncomfortable and a cause of distress when this is accompanied by insults, bullying, and prejudice (Glick et al., 2007).

2.2.2 Family, Home and School

Autobiographical texts by gay men and films and TV shows about gay men have often highlighted the difficulties they faced while growing up in homes and families and attending schools which they felt misunderstood them or pressured them to 'man up'. Some of these narratives – such as the films *Reinventing Marvin* (2017) and *Everybody's Talking About Jamie* (2021) – will be explored in the chapters to follow, so I will limit my comment here to general observations.

It's undoubtedly the case that gender-nonconforming boys still experience effeminophobia in domestic spaces, although attitudes towards gender-nonconforming people in the West have changed enormously since John's letter to *ONE* magazine in 1963. But nevertheless, as the narratives in this book demonstrate, there are long-lasting psychological traumas associated with being considered insufficiently masculine and hence a likely homosexual in a space in which a male's masculinity is paramount.

In Richard Green's landmark 1987 study of *sissy boys*, the parents who came to him often did so because they were aware that their sons were being bullied at school, but the situation at home was more complicated. Several of the mothers Green interviewed were actively encouraging of their son's femininity. One son explained to Green that he felt his mother 'pushed' him in a feminine direction because she sensed this was 'natural' for him: 'I would say from the age of walking and talking', he said, 'she's always sort of pushed me in the direction that she thought I would be successful or enjoy' (p. 80). Another son noted the close bond he had with his mother: 'there were times I'd tell her things because we had such a good relationship I just felt like I could tell her anything' (p. 81).

Green's non-judgemental approach to parents' behaviour meant that parents were able to open up about their fears surrounding their sons' effeminacy and possible homosexuality.[2] While some mothers wanted to encourage their sons, they also recognised, sometimes from the father's input, that teasing and bullying from their son's peers was having a negative impact, and that they had to try to stop it. Green shows that attempts to try to steer these *sissy boys* in a more masculine direction arose from complex motives and cannot be reduced to straightforward homophobia or even effeminophobia. As depicted in *Everybody's Talking About Jamie* (2021), which also demonstrates that Green's preoccupations are still relevant today, parental concern that their sons tone down their effeminacy are often rooted in parental solicitude for their boys' welfare at school, to protect them from hurt, and possibly also due to their own insecurities about having a sissy as a son.

This represents a realistic if somewhat unsatisfactory outcome, because while the boys might be more protected from bullying, it also means suppressing the boys' natural tendencies and capitulating to society's dominant standard for male behaviour. As the mother of 'Richard' said in her interview with Green when 'Richard' was aged 10, 'I feel very differently about him [now, from when he was younger]. He is okay. We shouldn't manipulate his environment.[3] His dignity has suffered [...] I can accept it if he becomes homosexual. It'll be all right. It won't reflect on me as a bad parent' (p. 228). In fact, 'Richard' grew up to be a heterosexual man.

More recent studies have shown that school spaces can still be challenging for gender-nonconforming boys, whether they identify as gay or not; a recent study of 449 Polish gay men even found that peer non-acceptance of childhood gender nonconformity was more closely linked to adult depressive symptoms and social anxiety than negative parental responses (Folkierska-Żukowska et al., 2022). C. J. Pascoe's 2007 study of masculinity and sexuality in a US high school showed that, according to the schoolchildren themselves, the label *fag* was used by children to police implicitly *heterosexual* peers' behaviour. Boys who were suspected of actually *being* a 'faggot' were in fact shielded from torrents of abuse or what Pascoe refers to as 'fag discourse'.

However, Pascoe's story of 'Ricky' contests this narrative and is particularly moving. 'Ricky's' experience at River High was marked by what seemed to be an institutional culture of fag-bashing: 'Ricky embodied the fag because of his homosexuality and his less normative gender identification and self-presentation', explains Pascoe (2012, p. 65). For 'Ricky', his sexuality was immediately recognised by peers and he was frequently asked to out himself by peers who already knew the answer to their question before they asked it. Contrary to what the other pupils said about only targeting those they assumed were not in fact gay, 'Ricky' was subject to continual harassment at school.

Sadly, 'Ricky' came to the point of admitting that, 'in a weird way, I'm comfortable with it because it's just what I've known for as long as I can remember. I mean, in elementary school [...] I started being called a fag. Fifth grade I was called a fag. Third grade I was called a fag' (p. 67). 'Ricky' eventually dropped out of River High: 'His double transgression of sexual and gender identity made his position at River High simply unliveable. The abuse that was heaped on him was more than one person, certainly more than one parentless, undereducated, sweet, artistic adolescent, could bear' (p. 71).

Other studies have highlighted more positive treatment of non-normative gender and sexuality in schools, so perhaps the tide is turning, in some places, at some moments (McCormack, 2012). But 'Ricky's' story shows how difficult it can be in school for a boy who simply cannot hide his effeminacy and latent homosexuality. When institutional spaces and cultures fail to address discrimination and bullying under their purview, it becomes 'unliveable', as Pascoe says (echoing Butler), for someone who is not only *a* fag, but *the* fag, as they bear the brunt of adolescent insecurity and malice, which more often than not the institution cannot or will not face up to. Belonging in such a space can be extremely challenging if not nigh on impossible. And, as I will demonstrate in Chapter 4, by focusing only on combating homophobia, the messier realities of bullying targeted at gender nonconformity and gay effeminacy remain ignored.

2.2.3 The LGBTQ+/Gay 'Community'

Until very recently, the 'LGBTQ+ community' and even the 'gay community' were thoroughly Western, middle-class and politicised concepts. But even in the West, it's only since the Second World War that there has been any self-consciously collective self-awareness in which homosexuals, defined as men who are attracted to the same sex, sought *each other* as desirable sexual partners. Quentin Crisp's memoir, *The Naked Civil Servant* (1985), for example, demonstrates that at least until the interwar years in London, effeminate gay men, (*queans*), like Chauncey's interwar American *fairies*, sought to form exogamous or heterogender unions or encounters with 'normal' or 'real' men, often called *trade* (Houlbrook, 2005).

This is a pattern which, until 40 or 50 years ago, also had significant cross-cultural parallels (Murray, 2000). But as the *homosexual* and *heterosexual* became used as terms to denote men separated by sexual object choice (see Chapter 1) homosexual men were increasingly forced to select sexual and romantic partners from within their own 'queer' community (Loftin, 2007;

Plummer, 1963). As Gert Hekma has said of a similar shift occurring in Holland at the same time, this amounted to a transition from 'sissies looking for straight guys to gay men deliberately pursuing each other' (2014, p. 123).

One consequence of this shift is that, whereas before, only the effeminate, passive partner was considered homosexual and stigmatised as a result, now, *any* male who had sex with another male ran the risk of being seen as effeminate and homosexual. As Hekma, Oosterhuis, and Steakley have noted, this meant that 'working-class men who might earlier have been engaged in homosexual practices on their own terms were now dishonoured even if they took the active role' (1995, p. 28). For some queens, pansies and fairies, they could no longer access 'real men' who would want to fuck them: self-identified homosexuals had to select partners from among their own community, with its own internal anxieties about insufficient masculinity and scarcity of 'real men'.

The rise of the 'clone' in the 1970s, or the overtly macho gay man, coincides with this 'butch shift', because in a sense the clone not only represented a hyper-masculinisation of gay men who rejected the slender and effete queen, swish, or pansy image, it was also adopted by gay men in order to be attractive to other gay men who could no longer attract a self-identified masculine 'heterosexual' (Levine, 1998). 'By the 1980s', writes Houlbrook, 'the "obvious" quean had given way to the invisible "homosexual"' (2005, p. 163). Where, previously, effeminate gay men in Britain and North America had been able to select masculine 'normal' men known as *trade*, they now had to select partners from among themselves, following the pattern of the middle-class, homosexually identified *queers*. This led to increased attempts to look more masculine – such as dressing differently and becoming more muscular – in order to attract masculine men (Cole, 2000; Stines, 2017). For some homosexuals, this shift to the masculine was welcome and in accord with their own felt sense of gender; for others, it often felt artificial – a mask hiding the fact that they were *not* like the 'real men' they could no longer access (Loftin, 2007). Indeed, the clone image can even be seen as another form of drag or an overt gender performance. As one informant told Martin Levine, 'Darling [. . .] beneath all this butch drag, we are still girls' (Levine, 1998, p. 63).

This shift from a largely exogamous and heterogender pattern of partner selection to an endogamous and egalitarian one has had significant implications for belonging and marginalisation among those gay men who either refuse to or cannot defeminise and masculinise but who remain locked within the gay/LGBTQ+ community by virtue of their sex object choice. They are routinely touted as undesirable sexual partners for other gay men – as indeed Crisp said of his fellow *queans*, and as many scholars studying non-Western effeminate bottoms have also noted: they are not, on the whole, attracted to each other or to a fem–fem dynamic (Murray, 2000; Prieur, 1998; Ravenhill & de Visser, 2018). There is therefore likely to be some truth when gay men say that, with exceptions, they do not find effeminate gay men attractive. Such men, like the effeminate gay men they find unattractive, typically seek masculine partners.

The problem is that only the former are willing or able to transform themselves, with varying degrees of success (like John who wrote to *ONE*), into the kind of partner they seek and who will therefore choose them as a partner as well; the effeminate gay men do not, and so become the marginalised among the marginalised but can no longer generally access sexual or romantic 'straight man' partners outside the gay/LGBTQ+ community (Taywaditep, 2002). Fernández-Alemany and Murray have noted in this respect:

> *How to create a society that will accept homosexual people not by trying to change them into masculine gay clones but by accepting gender nonconformity and the multiple ways of being gay as valid is a difficult question – one that has not been answered by the gay and lesbigay movements in the north.* (2002, p. 166)

The persistent point in this question is how to emphasise the variety of ways to be gay. Gender nonconformity is certainly discussed with increasing frequency, but not on the whole as a way to be gay or same-sex attracted. Issues of gender nonconformity tend to be detached from issues of sexual orientation and treated as phenomena to be dealt with independently under the rubric of 'gender identity'. While this manoeuvre might be suitable for some, it may inadvertently limit perceptions of what it means to be gay.

Early gay scholars such as Joseph Harry showed how, in any case, effeminate boys who become adult gay men tend to defeminise to some extent during adolescence, either due to the effect of puberty and increased circulating testosterone, or due to peer pressure – gay or otherwise – to appear acceptable to others and pretend that their sexual orientation is the only thing differentiating them from straight men (1983). This is why, for instance, some gay men recollect more childhood gender nonconformity than adult gender nonconformity – because they have, by and large, defeminised by adulthood – or, at least, they are able to 'turn it on and off' at will depending on environment. But it's self-identified bottoms rather than versatiles or tops that are likely to have defeminised to a lesser extent or who have been unable or unwilling to defeminise at all since childhood (Swift-Gallant et al., 2021). Pascoe's story of 'Ricky' illustrates an effeminate boy who was unable to defeminise during adolescence and was subsequently bullied for his persistent sexual and gender nonconformity.

The gay and wider LGBTQ+ community can therefore be a space of marginalisation for effeminate gay men and fem bottoms, from which they are largely forced to select their romantic and sexual partners. But many gay men will not find them attractive because effeminate bottoms remind them of what they might have been had they not, to varying degrees, defeminised. Equally, fem bottoms may have a hard time finding the kind of traditionally masculine or macho man they might have previously had sexual access to in a different historical era, and similarly, the kind of men potentially interested in fem bottoms and a heterogender dynamic may be put off interacting with them because they don't want to be seen as effeminate as well.

The irony is – as I will explore in Chapter 5 – contemporary fem bottoms such as *pussyboys* and *boiwives* are only too happy to be seen as the fem one in a heterogender union, and are keen to preserve the masculine self-image of their top partners. Indeed, most fem bottoms don't *want* the same as them. But sadly, the current cultural emphasis on sex object choice identities – being same-sex attracted – is enough to conceal these nuances in sexual aim, leading to feelings of marginalisation and frustration from both fem bottoms and the men who may be attracted to them (Vytniorgu, 2024a).

2.2.4 Online Spaces

Some of the narratives explored in this book are found online, particularly from social media platforms such as Tumblr and Reddit. These platforms enable spaces in which LGBTQ+-identified people and non-LGBTQ+-identified people can connect with others, discover more about their desires and fantasies, and imagine a sense of belonging in some of the other places and spaces explored in this chapter. For example, fem bottoms who have hitherto been unable to find romantic or sexual partners offline, may discover a community in which their sexual and gender presentation is attractive – perhaps to bisexual men or men who do not (want to) identify as gay at all.

The role of online erotica and pornography is significant in this process. As I will show, some of the key narratives associated with effeminate bottoms on pornographic and erotic platforms situate these bottoms in the context of the home and school, where they are no longer objects of prejudice and abuse, but desired by other men and are able to be among other bottoms like them. Sites such as Tumblr, Twitter/X, and Reddit act as mediating spaces for effeminate belonging. For some, this is connected to a wider sexual fantasy realm, in which *faggot* is no longer a term of abuse used by non-gay people towards gay males, but a term of self-chosen (dis)empowerment fuelled by erotic desire. As such, online users are able to create what media scholars refer to as a 'counterpublic' in which marginalised or disenfranchised individuals come together to imagine new forms of belonging on their own terms (Warner, 2002). Digital worlds can therefore also represent 'queer utopias' in which LGBTQ+ people can meet, share experiences, opinions, and fantasies, and also offer mutual support that can help them offline, too (Muñoz, 2009; Shaw & Sender, 2016).

When Tumblr announced its crackdown on adult content in December 2018, this led to a palpable sense of anxiety among users who relied on Tumblr to build connections and share content, and they were left wondering where to go. Many users who had blogs with followers in the thousands fled to Twitter/X, and others to a new microblogging platform, BDSMlr. The rise of OnlyFans has also meant that the line between amateur erotica and porn and professional porn is blurred; for some of these actors/models, more well-known social media such as Twitter/X and Instagram are used as calling card sites to drive traffic to their OnlyFans accounts. Equally, porn sites such as XVideos, XHamster and BoyfriendTV enable a community of people to comment and create video playlists around their preferred content. For effeminate bottoms, this means that the figure of the fem bottom can be elevated to a place of relative respect and desire, which can contrast radically with their reception by others in offline contexts. However, there are limits to acceptable gender nonconformity, even on online spaces such as these. As I will show in my analysis of comments around gay porn actors (Chapter 5), if a bottom is too effeminate or faggy, even if he has an otherwise desirable body, they are rejected by viewers as crossing unacceptable boundaries.

2.3 BELONGING TO A STIGMATISED IDENTITY

I have begun to suggest that effeminate belonging is multifaceted. It is not straightforwardly positive. One can belong to abusive names, such as Pascoe's 'Ricky', who seemed to internalise his name-calling to such an extent that he had normalised it. He had effectively come to belong with being the school *fag*. One can also belong to normalised ideas of appropriate occupation for an effeminate gay man and fem bottom: either as something stereotypical like a hairdresser, or else as a sex worker whose only worth seems to be to take the dick of 'real men'. To echo Stephen Murray's analysis, their main role is to be a 'male receptacle for phallic discharges' (2000, p. 255). While this may suit some effeminate bottoms – and has historically been and still is in some places the main or only role for such males – it may also be extremely uncomfortable for others.

As I see it, the main issue is that, unlike so-called 'straight-acting' gay men, effeminate gay men, and fem bottoms in particular, are generally unable to conceal their sexuality and gender nonconformity even if they adopt patterns of code-switching (Eguchi, 2009). Their stigmatised identity precedes any disclosure, which means that the communication of their identity is often at the hands of others, who use uncongenial language in uncongenial tones (recall my own childhood experience in the Introduction). For those like 'Ricky', who cannot hide their effeminate homosexuality, it's possible to come to belong to a distorted understanding of its possibilities as an identity. The problem is not that these males conform to stereotypes, but that these stereotypes become sources of prejudice and marginalisation. In other words, it's fine (and realistic) to conform to a type, but it is not fine when conforming to type is made to seem pathological, deviant, and *wrong* (Norton, 2016). Those men – many of whom are gay/LGBTQ+ themselves – who criticise the conflation of effeminacy and bottoming are thus as culpable as those non-gay people who simply find in a fem gay a target of derision.

Online spaces, on the other hand, as well as films and other fictional work, may afford fem bottoms new ways to imagine and communicate a sense of belonging – to take ownership of it themselves and adjust how they see themselves. I would suggest that nude or erotic modelling, for example, is one performative way for effeminate bottoms to rediscover their own bodies, and to re-connect their gender-nonconforming personality with their embodied maleness (see Chapter 5). Creative and erotic practices like these seem to me to be important for negotiating embodied belonging, and another reason why, especially for gay men, the issue of the virtues or not of pornography and erotica seem to be fraught and complex (Mercer, 2017; Paasonen, 2011). For fem bottoms who consume online erotic content, they may be able to visualise new possibilities for their maleness beyond stereotypical masculinity, enabling them to re-orient themselves more confidently to offline encounters with men they desire.

But I must also ask why it is that erotica and porn have become such a key site of visibility for effeminate bottoms and the men who desire them. Can effeminate belonging *only* be built in this way? Is the sexual aspect of their identity sometimes over-emphasised, or even misinterpreted (as a kink), at the expense of non-sexual aspects of being gender nonconforming? And, is there a risk that some fem bottoms who circulate sexual fantasies online come to think of their fem bottom identity as a completely online, almost disembodied concept divorced from offline reality? Equally, what about the models who provide the erotic imagery? In such spaces, these bottoms may, like the non-Western ones described above, be encouraged to think of their bodies as their main source of economic capital – indeed, perhaps even their main source of self-worth – and it would be desperately naïve to maintain that every model on OnlyFans or those who work for a gay porn studio do so for reasons of self-empowerment. Nevertheless, online platforms, whether erotic or not, have become increasingly salient for negotiating effeminate belonging among those who feel marginalised offline. I explore some of these questions in more detail in Chapter 5.

In the next chapter, I will outline the diversity of narratives to be explored in the second half of the book.

NOTES

1. See also work by cultural geographers working in the fields of emotional geography, who have focused specifically on how place mediates emotional experiences of belonging (Fenton et al., 2012; Pile, 2010). Andrew Gorman-Murray has also examined how gay men negotiate the physical space of home (2008; Gorman-Murray & Cook, 2020).
2. Green's work has nevertheless received criticism for inadequately equipping effeminate boys to handle the masculinising impetus of gay activism on the one hand, and medicalising discourses of effeminacy on the other (Piontek, 2006, pp. 55–57).
3. Names of participants in social scientific studies which narrate life stories are put in quotation marks to emphasise the constructed nature of them as narrative protagonists, driving a narrative forward (see Smith & Watson, 2010, pp. 71–76).

3

NARRATIVES ON THE MARGINS

This chapter briefly introduces the corpus of narratives to be explored in Part Two and indicates the significance of the narrative genres selected, as situating experiences of gender nonconformity and bottom identities on the margins of contemporary LGBTQ+ media. The narratives selected are by no means exhaustive in coverage, but they do indicate some key genres and media in which bottom identities and gender nonconforming experience are represented and explored in the contemporary moment.

These narratives encompass the fictional and non-fictional, the visual, written and aural, and are circulated online and offline. They are also fairly recent. Most of the narratives selected for discussion were produced since 2007, with the majority being produced since 2010. Narratives were selected on the basis of trying to include a range of generic vantage points (poetry, film, photo journalism, documentary, online porn, written erotica, etc.), a range of geographical places that enable contextualisation of Anglo-American and Western with non-Western, and which explore belonging and marginalisation in places and spaces relevant to this book, such as home, family, school, LGBTQ+ community and online.

Inevitably, the selection is not exhaustive and is personal to me as well – a reality routinely accepted in fields such as literary and cultural studies because of their embrace of the interpersonal identification with the known, but still sometimes viewed with suspicion in more positivist fields that demand discourses of methodology that can exhaust themselves when it comes to creative work, especially online (Mousley, 2013; Palmer, 1993). As cultural theorist Raymond Williams originally recognised in relation to television, engagement with cultural and creative forms such as film, TV and even online porn and its paratexts must recognise the affective and sequential states in which this material can be encountered, encouraging a sense of flow that is open to surprises and serendipity (Arroyo, 2016; Williams, 2003).

Or, as literary critic and theorist Andy Mousley has written, it's important to recognise the way in which texts can be brought together through what he terms 'purposeful wandering' and what literary theorist Rita Felski has termed a text's 'sociability', resonating with the reader's or viewer's own internal sense of meaning-making that can be resistant to the kind of scrutiny often demanded by positivist scholars (Felski, 2011; Mousley, 2013, p. 10; see also Vytniorgu, 2019). In relation to a book on gay bottom identities such as this, sense of flow can be even more specific. As rhetoric scholar Timothy Oleksiak has suggested, composing, or writing 'as a bottom', can involve taking a bottom's 'stance', demonstrating 'openness to the pleasures that are found in what is offered' by way of texts, images and media (2022, p. 360).

Moreover, the term *narrative* itself is also porous: a beginning, middle and end, are too simplistic to account for the diversity and complexity of ways in which the narratives explored in this book structure events and experiences – something that social scientists interested in 'narrative analysis' also recognise (Weatherhead, 2011). Often it is a fleeting moment, a re-constructed traumatic memory or a fantasy of desire that may be imagined through physical response and stimulation, which constitute the narratives explored. As Gubrium and Holstein argue, 'narratives need not be full-blown stories with requisite internal structures'; they may be fragmented and piecemeal (1997, p. 146).

Framing devices, unreliable, hesitant or multiple narrators and protagonists, as well as online commentators who single out aspects of a visual or moving story for criticism or praise, also underscore the variety of ways in which narrative is approached. Certainly, when it comes to the autobiographical narrative, it may well be more nuanced to talk of *autobiographical acts*, as suggested by Sidonie Smith and Julia Watson, which would recognise the range of components that make up an autobiographical act, including media, audiences, paratextual frames and sites, as well as emplotment (2010, p. 64; Vytniorgu, 2024a). While welcoming the diversity of narratives out there, there are still key features that characterise a form of communication as narrative, including the emergence of voice through story, and the attachment of meaning and form to events, experiences, and the development of identity. Attention to these aspects permeates my readings of a diverse range of sources.

As the book has progressed, however, it has also become clear that, while it's still useful to think in terms of texts and narratives, it's also advisable, from a media angle, to consider texts and narratives in conjunction with practices of automediality, or the ways in which people 'live in relationship with media' (Kennedy & Maguire, 2018, n.p.; Moser, 2019). In other words, I wish to consider how sexual experiences are not only represented by media but how they are also shaped by how people experience and engage with digital media in the process of consolidating their sexual identities and practices (see also Poletti & Rak, 2014). This is especially pertinent for Chapter 5, which explores paratexts around gay porn uploads and image-text posts on microblogging platforms such as Tumblr and Twitter/X.

Not all of the narratives selected for inclusion in this book will be commented on individually in close readings: some will be grouped together to explore key themes over the following chapters. The material is also largely divided into non-erotic, which is the focus of Chapter 4, and the erotic and pornographic, which is the focus of Chapter 5. This division is inevitably a little arbitrary, but for the sake of this book, the erotic and pornographic are those narratives which are primarily devoted to this kind of content rather than being incidental.

3.1 NON-EROTIC NARRATIVES

These narratives can be divided into five main genres: fictional film and TV drama, non-fictional documentaries, LGBTQ+ forum commentary, animation, music videos and photo journalism and other visual imagery.

The films *The Blossoming of Maximo Oliveros* (Philippines, 2005), *Everybody's Talking About Jamie* (UK, 2021), *Reinventing Marvin* (France, 2017) and the TV drama *It's a Sin* (UK, 2020) all dramatically highlight the tensions at play in different places and spaces for belonging as a gender nonconforming same-sex attracted male across Western and non-Western places and spaces. *Everybody's Talking About Jamie* and *Reinventing Marvin* focus explicitly on the experiences of bullying and marginalisation caused by men in the protagonists' lives who read them as effeminate, probably gay and somehow a failure in the home/family and school spaces. These narratives emphasise the difficulties these young men face in being a 'sissy boy' and, to echo Pascoe's study of 'Ricky' discussed in Chapter 2, also being the high school 'fag', or at least read as such by others.[1] By contrast, *The Blossoming of Maximo Oliveros* presents a situation of growing up as gender nonconforming in a male-dominated space but shows the possibility for a more sympathetic acceptance of an effeminate boy who is able to belong in the home and family in such a way that he is able to openly express himself and even be protected by his brothers and fathers who defend his difference.

As a genre, documentaries are immensely useful in pinpointing cultural preoccupations and perspectives on gender and sexuality issues, although they are not as prominent in the cultural sphere as fictional films and TV. For this reason, *Effeminate Belonging* devotes relatively more space to discussing documentaries than to fictional film and TV. All the documentaries under consideration here deal with the fraught question of how far same-sex attraction is imbricated with gender nonconformity or being effeminate, particularly if bottoming or being a bottom is also taken into consideration. These documentaries therefore underscore cultural interest in the themes discussed in Chapter 1, such as the relationship between sexual aim and sexual object. The Anglophone documentary, *Olly Alexander: Growing up Gay* (UK, 2017), demonstrates uneasiness with suggesting that marginalisation experienced by gay men and boys is often caused by effeminophobia rather than homophobia, thereby cementing a link between effeminacy and homosexuality that the UK and US LGBTQ+ cultural contexts in which these documentaries were created would rather forget or diminish in importance.

By contrast, *Samantha Hudson* (Spain, 2018) and *Being Male, Being Kothi* (India, 2010) deal more frankly with the issue of gender nonconforming experience among same-sex attracted males. The Spanish documentary about a young drag queen (also known as Iván Gonzalez Ranedo) draws almost diametrically opposed conclusions about effeminacy and homosexuality to *Olly Alexander: Growing up Gay*, and the film, *Everybody's Talking About Jamie*. For Hudson (born 1999), who also produced a 2015 song entitled 'Maricón' [trans. *faggot*], belonging with effeminacy and a bottom subjectivity is intimately connected to their expression of being gay. Meanwhile, the Indian documentary, *Being Male, Being Kothi* highlights the tension between indigenous identities associated with being an effeminate bottom, and Western identities that aim to separate sexual orientation from gender expression and sex role. Paul Harfleet's British book and animation, *Pansy Boy* (UK, 2017), also takes a more positive approach to the connection between gender nonconformity and being gay and highlights his effeminacy as one of the main reasons he was bullied in his school. For Harfleet, *pansy* has become a word to reclaim, thereby demonstrating a shift in belonging discussed in Chapter 2, to taking positive ownership of words that other people have used to define oneself in negative ways.

In the music industry, the English-speaking singer most associated in recent years with being gay and with bottoming is the Australian-South African singer and songwriter, Troye Sivan (born 1995), whose 2018 single 'Bloom' trended on Twitter/X under the hashtag #BopsBoutBottoming. Since then, Sivan has courted speculation about his gay sex preference, which he refuses to discuss outside his music. Nevertheless, music videos such as 'Angel Baby' (2021) and 'Lucky Strike' (2019) openly imagine Sivan as somewhat gender nonconforming, in contrast to more masculine bodies in the videos who act as objects of Sivan's desire. In Chapter 4, I will consider the extent to which Sivan's music videos create a space for belonging with effeminacy at the same time as courting, even if not disclosing, a gay bottom identity. By contrast, Brazilian singer Gabeu (Gabriel Silva Felizardo, born 1998) has, like Hudson, visibly courted synergies between effeminacy and bottom subjectivity and has re-imagined rural spaces as those in which *pocs* – effeminate bottoms – find fulfilment.

Other visual, non-erotic material to be analysed includes Candace Feit's 2015 photo journalism narrative, *A Woman in My Heart*, exploring the identities of Indian *kothis*. I will also be exploring the role of media such as Data Lounge and Reddit, which allow users to explore anxieties about effeminacy, bottoming and ageing, as well as circulating sexual fantasy narratives that imagine the sex roles of celebrities based on gender conforming or nonconforming traits. These forums also bridge the erotic and non-erotic.

3.2 EROTIC AND PORNOGRAPHIC NARRATIVES

Since the 1990s, the critical study of pornography has increased rapidly and is now understood to be a valid and important field of academic inquiry in the broader interdisciplinary area of the visual arts, culture and media, as testified by the journal *Porn Studies*, which launched in 2014. Initial, groundbreaking work focused largely on heterosexual pornography, particularly the work of Linda Williams (1989), while the work of Richard Dyer and Thomas Waugh spearheaded interest in gay porn (Dyer, 1985, 1990; Waugh, 1996), with John Mercer's 2017 *Gay Pornography: Representations of Sexuality and Masculinity* constituting a thorough assertion of the value and insight attached to gay porn for wider issues in the study of gender and sexuality (see also Florêncio, 2020; Wignall, 2022). Recently, gay porn scholars have broadened their attention beyond the study of studio-produced porn to what Sharif Mowlabocus has termed 'Porn 2.0', or porn which is self-made and circulates on social media (2010), and thereby demands that the concept of media itself is interrogated as it seeks to represent, shape and actively transform sexual identities, behaviours and practices.

Fem gays are rarely foregrounded in Western studio-produced gay porn in any positive way, and as I argue in Chapter 5 in relation to Tannor Reed and

Bar Addison, when a model does speak or behave in an effeminate manner, many viewers are likely to be put off or even repulsed. Outside mainstream gay porn produced by Western-focused studios such as Cocky Boys, BelAmi or Sean Cody, there is more willingness to entertain effeminate gender presentations among models and actors, particularly among twinks.

Once one moves beyond Western-centric studios, there is more latitude for exploring diverse gendered presentations among models and actors that embrace effeminate bottoms. Latin American companies such as M2M Club (Argentina) write about their videos in English but tend to present stark contrasts between tops and bottoms in ways reminiscent of the literature exploring Latin American homosexualities noted in Chapters 1 and 2. In M2M Club, for example, bottoms are often simply called *fags* or *faggots*, indicating a convergence of sexual orientation, anal sex role as bottoms and gender expression as non-*macho*. They are not simply *bottoms*: they are *faggots*. The model named Ezebaires, for example, is variously referred to as *sissy, effeminate, pussy-boy, bottom fag, effeminate fag, passive fag* and a *sub bottom 'twink'* (M2M Club). Moreover, unlike Western studios such as FamilyDick, M2M Club does not restrict itself to models and actors who tend to be under 30; their *faggots* are often over 30.

The erotic and pornographic material explored in this book aims to show the extent to which gay porn and erotica on the margins speak to interest in effeminate bottom identities as well as the identities of those who desire them. The approach taken to the study of gay porn and erotica here is to focus largely on paratexts produced in relation to studio-produced porn and to read content on social media 'microblogging' sites such as Tumblr, Twitter/X and Reddit, and written erotica on websites such as Gay Spiral Stories that sometimes fuse the fictional and the autobiographical. Tumblr and Twitter/X represent online spaces in which users can share sexual fantasies and communicate with one another in both a 'one-to-many' and a 'one-to-one' format, via Direct Message, and thus begin to build some sort of community around gender nonconforming experience.[2]

Media scholars have coined the term *automediality* to describe the ways in which online users craft content that is also a form of self-fashioning, moving away from concepts such as *autobiography* which do not adequately explain how self-representation occurs online. Rather, automediality emphasises self-representation as 'a cultural practice of subjectivization that, depending on historical circumstances, makes use of various media, often in the form of multimodal combinations' (Moser, 2019, p. 257). Tumblr and Twitter/X enable users to combine visual material and written captions, as well as adding (hash)tags that can stimulate erotic fantasy as well as linking these posts to others that may also entice.

The written erotica on Gay Spiral Stories and Menonthenet.com explores 'the view from the bottom' (Jennings, 2005, pp. 70–71; Nguyen, 2014), particularly the desires, identities and subjectivity of fem bottoms who often relish the opportunity to transform more masculine men into 'fairies' or fem twinks like themselves, sometimes referred to as 'twinkification', such as in the stories 'From Bear to Fair (-y)' (2008) and 'SHORT: Seeds of a Twink Variety' (2016). These stories reclaim slurs and words which have historically been directed at gender nonconforming boys in the home and school (such as *fairy* and *fag*) and write them in ways that emphasise their ability to label a positive sense of gay bottom identity. Other stories, such as the story published on Menonthenet.com by Greg, 'Pussyboy' (2001), offer an extended meditation on the development and transformation of 'a real twink' into a proudly effeminate bottom who has found a sense of belonging in a heterogender relationship with a masculine top.

Focusing on written erotica as well as visual material circulated on Tumblr and Twitter/X also involves a focus on paratexts such as (hash)tags and descriptions, which tend to inform a broader discourse around effeminate bottoms that also circulates on subreddits such as r/TopsAndBottoms. In r/TopsAndBottoms (122k members), bottoms and tops find a place of belonging and sanctuary from more popular gay subreddits such as r/askgaybros (433k members), which tends to resist the 'heteronormative' equation of effeminacy and bottom subjectivity (Vytniorgu, 2024a). For example, one user commented on r/askgaybros:

> *Nothing turns me off more than fem guys. Most fem guys I run into tend to be a combination of small, lean, hairless, dress flamboyantly, act over the top dramatic, lack ambition and want to be coddled and 'taken care of'. They are also almost always pure, greedy bottoms. No thanks. I want nothing to do with that. I'm just a normal dude who leans more towards masc. I don't want to feel embaressed* [sic] *in public with my dude, I don't think that's unreasonable.*

The value judgement placed on 'most fem guys' here is clear in its negative connotations: fem is equated with being a 'pure, greedy bottom', which is bad, in the eyes of this user. In r/TopsAndBottoms, by contrast, users find a more welcoming space for belonging with more gender complementary or heterogender relationships, where it's obvious who the bottom is in a relationship: they are not embarrassed to be seen with a guy who is obviously read by others as a fem bottom. As one user opined on Reddit: 'I want to jerk off to real, fabulous, gay as fuck, effeminate, beautiful faggots. Not sissies or crossdressers. Just your pretty looking stereotypical fag bottom boy, with silky hair, smooth skin, clean shaven... the "gay mannerisms" and every thing!'. Reddit therefore functions as a mediator of erotic and pornographic discourse that finds visual expression on other social media apps such as Tumblr and Twitter/X. Language describing fem bottoms appears with more frequency in r/TopsAndBottoms than r/askgaybros, and users regularly post narratives that fantasise about masc–fem relationships that elsewhere on Reddit may be rejected as anachronistic.

Concerns about being 'read' as effeminate or as a bottom by others also highlight the overall significance of reading in what follows in the rest of the book. One of the chief achievements of cultural studies has been to expand the kind of content that can be considered worthy of study, embracing film, 'popular' TV, fashion, buildings, bodies – even the anus itself (Allan, 2016). The autobiographical is at the heart of this connection: narratives in this book which are created in autobiographical ways often draw attention to how the autobiographical narrative is borne out of being 'read' in ways that are sometimes hard to assimilate into one's identity. For example, the French film *Reinventing Marvin* utilises autobiographical framing devices to emphasise the emotional difficulties inherent in how Marvin has been 'read' in gendered and sexual ways by others. The film's autobiographical narrative focuses on Marvin's quest to reclaim modes of reading the self in ways that are respectful, creative and which develop a sense of belonging. Of course, as Susanna Paasonen has argued, in cultural studies, reading must often be accompanied by other acts as well: viewing, touching, feeling – all of which gesture at a life-affirming role for cultural studies that has often been eclipsed by a negativity associated with cultural critique (2011).

Taken together, both the non-erotic and erotic/pornographic narratives selected for discussion indicate the range and diversity of exploration into gender nonconforming experience and gay bottom identities that simultaneously expand what we think of as narrative, to include practices of automediality that highlight the ways in which subjects 'live in relationship with media' (Kennedy & Maguire, 2018, n.p.). Moreover, the creative nature of many of these narratives also necessitates a flexible attitude to lived experience. As autobiography scholars have long-argued, life narratives that are artfully re-arranged may be departing from 'the truth' or 'authenticity', if accessing these were ever possible in the first place. But in re-imagining experiences and identities from a standpoint of agency, the autobiographical nature of these narratives may embody a different, more relevant kind of integrity (Lejeune, 1989; Smith & Watson, 2010).

The majority of the narratives are Western (principally produced in the United Kingdom and the United States), but reference to non-Western and global majority narratives serves to contextualise preoccupations in the West and to put these into perspective. Those narratives which currently sit on the margins in the West, such as heterogender fantasies, may be placed more centrally in non-Western depictions of same-sex desire and experience.

In the next chapter, I focus on how non-erotic narratives negotiate the relationships between sexual orientation (being same-sex attracted), gender expression (being effeminate) and sex role preference (being a bottom) and ask whether these narratives suggest it is possible or even desirable to belong as all three: a fem gay bottom.

NOTES

1. The 2008 BBC comedy series *Beautiful People*, based on the memoirs of Simon Doonan, also depict the early adolescence of an effeminate boy in a British school told from the perspective of his older effeminate gay self.

2. When my article, 'Effeminate Gay Bottoms in the West: Narratives of Pussyboys and Boiwives on Tumblr' was published online in 2022 in *Journal of Homosexuality*, the article was quickly liked and shared on Tumblr (over 1,800 notes within 2 months of publication) among accounts with a focus on gender nonconformity. This is perhaps somewhat unusual for academic publications but suggests that online users on Tumblr are interested in discussions of their communities and identities. In the tradition of cultural studies, it also highlights the porous relationship between cultural studies academics and the 'cultural sphere'.

Part 2

READINGS, CONCERNS AND DIRECTIONS

4

FEM GAY BOTTOM: CAN I BE ALL THREE?

Chapter 4 focuses on the ways in which the narratives introduced in Chapter 3 negotiate the relationship between gender expression (as fem or effeminate), sex object choice (attraction to men) and sex role (as a bottom). This chapter shows how, in practice, it is difficult to isolate any of these and turn them into a single organising principle for understanding issues to do with these subjects' gender-sexuality. LGBTQ+ media in the West frequently tries to detach gender expression from sex role, and there are good reasons for this, as many gay men do not want to feel constrained by what they consider to be unhelpful stereotypes such as the *effeminate bottom*. But this impetus has an adverse effect on those males who do fit the stereotype of the fem bottom and want to find ways to belong with this in more positive ways.

This chapter explores how these three elements of identity intersect, while offering a comparative stance by contextualising Western narratives with non-Western ones. The chapter argues that experiences of marginalisation can occur when there is pressure for effeminate males to defeminise, emphasise their sexual orientation over their sex/gender role positionality and to consider bottoming as a verb that one does, rather than a noun that one is and can belong to.

4.1 GENDER DISPLACED: EFFEMINACY AND DEFEMINISATION

In 2005, Paul Harfleet began planting pansies in places where a homophobic attack occurred. Since then, throughout the United Kingdom and further afield in cities such as Berlin, New York and Stockholm, Harfleet has overseen the planting of pansies in places that were once sites of bullying and prejudice targeted at those assumed to be gay (Harfleet, 2015). His illustrated children's book, *Pansy Boy* (2017), uses poetry to narrate the story at the core of what became the Pansy Project (www.thepansyproject.com). The book was subsequently animated with a narration from Harfleet. As a depiction of an effeminate boy's struggles with his peers, the book sits within a genre of *sissy boy* narratives, which in addition to the narratives explored below, also include more comedic representations such as the 2008 BBC comedy series *Beautiful People*, and which explore the challenges of boys who behave in ways considered by others to be effeminate and latently gay.

Written to his 7-year-old self, *Pansy Boy* tells the story of a young boy from 'an average town' who is bullied at school because of his effeminacy. 'His stance and demeanour may have been fey', explains the speaker in rhyming couplets, 'His nature girlish and potentially gay' (n.p.). Harfleet depicts the boy as slender, with a diamond/heart-shaped face, large eyes and high forehead, arched eyebrows, prominent cheekbones, and short but wavy hair swept off the forehead. He is dressed in a soft aesthetic, with woollen jumpers and flowing scarves. The boy's physical presence seems intended to underscore his difference to his fellow pupils, who seem physically more imposing, perhaps befitting their role as 'schoolboy tyrants'.

The effect of the boy's non-masculine physical presence and the speaker's description of his effeminate personality help to contextualise the speaker's insistence that 'It's not as though he had a say/It was always clear he was born this way'. For Harfleet, the pansy boy was born 'fey', 'girlish' and 'potentially gay', with a clear suggestion that the boy's effeminacy is a prelude to his later status as gay. This then explains why the Pansy Project as a whole is intended to combat homophobia, with its explicit reference to homosexuality. *Pansy Boy* therefore aligns squarely with the current scholarly consensus that sustained gender nonconformity in childhood is a strong predictor of adult homosexuality and is seen as such by other people (see Chapter 1).

For Harfleet's pansy boy, one of the main challenges faced by the boy is that the other children at school have the upper hand in defining who the boy is; they read him in ways that he struggles to absorb. 'Fairy, pansy or just queer were the words he came to fear', says the speaker. As with Pascoe's 'Ricky' in Chapter 2, Harfleet's pansy boy is forced to belong to words that are spoken in derogatory ways, and which shape his sense of self as being marginalised and different. The boy's response is to take ownership of these terms which describe his effeminacy and presumed gayness. At the back of the book Harfleet notes that the French etymology of *pansy* includes the sense of someone deep in thought. It's through reflection that the pansy boy comes to realise that he can plant pansies in 'locations layered with human woe'. At school, he plants 'pansies in the dirt', and eventually the teachers realise the meaning of the pansies, and the bullying eases. 'His modest plan to raise awareness', writes the speaker, 'increased the prospect of future fairness'.

Harfleet's *Pansy Boy* is a narrative that seeks to layer itself onto real-life stories of homophobic abuse, and by planting real pansies at sites of such abuse, Harfleet continues to assert the importance of reclaiming abusive language and re-reading situations so that it becomes something to belong to in life-affirming rather than destructive ways. Harfleet readily identifies himself on social media with *pansy*, and as such, echoes what 'dedicated bottom' Andrew Powles has said of his own story: 'They recognized and labelled something in me before I had managed to articulate it so I suppose they got the naming rights' (2003, p. 112). Harfleet is reclaiming these rights by re-identifying creatively with *pansy*.

Yet Harfleet's story is ultimately idealistic. It aims to change society and offer children a message of hope. Sadly, it is much more usual for boys who are effeminate to capitulate to the bullying and to seek to defeminise during adolescence in order to fit in – as I tried to do in my own adolescence (Harry, 1983; Taywaditep, 2002). Thus, rather than seeking to belong with effeminacy and create space for *pansy boys*, the aim is to displace it and reach a point where gender expression goes unnoticed, because it is read as sufficiently masculine. In this sense, *Pansy Boy* only tells half the story: it starts and ends in the pre-adolescent years where such optimism is perhaps more achievable because the challenges associated with puberty have yet to occur. Other narratives, such as the French film *Reinventing Marvin* (2017), continue the effeminate boy's story into adolescence and young adulthood, and depicts the difficulty and pain in defeminising due to stigma and internalised shame at not being sufficiently manly as someone whose body, on the face of it, is turning into that of a man.

Reinventing Marvin (French: *Marvin ou la belle éducation*) tells the story of a boy – presented as physically delicate but beautiful – aged 12 or 13, who is bullied at school and feels out of place at home due to his noticeable effeminacy. From the start of the film, we witness Marvin as the school *fag* (Pascoe, 2012): he is called *pédé* repeatedly and made fun of because of his surname – Bijou – which means jewel. He is read by one older boy in particular as being sexually receptive, even though he is still a boy, and is sexually assaulted by him in ways that are deliberately feminised: 'Don't change, Marvin', the older boy tells him, 'it's hot when you wiggle your ass. That's how we like you. Nice and girly' (0:12:43). Marvin lives in a rural village and his family is presented as firmly working class: his father drinks *pastis*, smokes and works as a refuse collector. Marvin's older step siblings also find him an anomaly, and his mother is blamed for making Marvin into a sissy. It's only when Marvin joins the school drama club that he begins to find a group of pupils among whom he can belong.

Echoing *The End of Eddy* by French novelist Édouard Louis (2014), *Reinventing Marvin* nuances the way in which the bullying affects Marvin's sense of belonging. While the scenes of verbal abuse and sexual assault, such as being made to fellate the bully after another bully applies lipstick to his lips, are unsettling, for Marvin they also awaken his sexual attraction to men, his gender nonconformity and identification with women, as well as his identification with sexually receptive roles. Through the use of a framing device, which recounts Marvin's youth through the autobiographical lens of a young adult Marvin, his adolescent development is focused on his difficult relationship to his own effeminacy: he struggles to belong with it. As a young adult, Marvin has defeminised to the extent that he is presented as fairly 'straight-acting' or typically masculine. By this time he has fled the rural neighbourhood of his boyhood and acculturated into a more middle-class metropolitan gay subculture.

One of the key developments in the narrative, however, is Marvin's sexual relationship with an older man – Roland – who not only wants to fuck Marvin, but seems to assume that this is something Marvin enjoys without Marvin telling him. This seems to reawaken insecurities on Marvin's part that he is read by others as insufficiently manly and as a sexually passive *pédé* – a realisation that troubles him, but also paradoxically excites him. Even as a 12-year-old, when recounting a scene of domestic abuse as part of a drama class exercise, Marvin subtly changes the language used against him: he replaces *pédé* (generic *faggot*), which is the word his father actually used against him, with *tapette* (signifying an effeminate *pansy* or *poof*), thereby strengthening his identification with effeminacy and sexual receptivity.

Reinventing Marvin shows how, quite understandably, Marvin defeminises from his 12-year-old effeminate self to a more-or-less masculine, unremarkable young man whose gender nonconformity has by this time been displaced: it's only his sexual orientation that stands out. Or, at least, mostly: he is still read by others as sexually receptive with an effeminate edge and, the film seems to suggest, even by Marvin himself at times. For Marvin, his emotional difficulties as an adult – conflicted about his sexuality and effeminacy – are mostly the result of his non-belonging as a child, at home and at school. In these places he is read as one of Harfleet's pansy boys. This is brought home to Marvin by a key speech made by adult Marvin's drama teacher:

> *Take a gay child [un enfant gay]. He's called a 'dirty faggot [pédé]', when he goes home, often no one offers support. No one consoles him. He's alone. So alone that he may not even mention it. Why? Because in his own home, in his own family, and often in a family that's culturally deprived, they insult faggots [pédale] and dykes. For me, this is a radical form of exile. That child, poor, sad, and gay, who I was, doesn't feel at home anywhere. He's a stranger in his own house, amid his own family. (1:18:35)*

Marvin responds emotionally to this speech, and it not only helps Marvin to reflect on himself and his difference, but also results in him distancing himself from his provincial roots which his teacher glosses as 'culturally deprived'. Later in the film, when Marvin produces a play based on his difficult childhood, his family is interviewed and his mother and sister are clearly upset by Marvin's *us and them* stance, treating them like 'retards [...] We're not homophobes', his mother insists (1:36:19-28). When he visits them towards the end of the film, Marvin explains that he was trying to 'save them all' through his play. But what this means is never made entirely clear.

What seems especially interesting, however, is that the character of Marvin Bijou and Paul Harfleet's pansy boy both seem to respond in broadly similar ways to early experiences of non-belonging in the home and at school. They turn to creativity to try and increase awareness of effeminophobic and homophobic attitudes and ultimately to eliminate these by reclaiming or re-reading a part of themselves that was initially moulded by the hands of others, sometimes in abusive ways. They are reclaiming the 'naming rights' to themselves (Powles, 2003, p. 112). In *Reinventing Marvin*, there is a sharp line drawn between Marvin's rural, boyhood neighbourhood and his acquired family in an urban, metropolitan centre with a recognisable gay subculture: the former is always on the back foot. And yet, at the end of the film, Marvin admits that he wants to 'come back. It's all I ever wanted' (1:42:38), and we see him for the last time in a rural setting, longing to belong in the place where, in spite of misunderstanding and abuse, he feels some attachment.

For Marvin, displacing his gender presentation and defeminising during adolescence seems to have been a defensive manoeuvre, designed to protect him from experiencing further abuse at the hands of others (Eguchi, 2009; Sánchez & Vilain, 2012). But one gets the feeling that, by the end of the film, Marvin would like to be with his family in the place where he grew up, to be himself without abuse. His older, experienced gay lover is removed from the scene somewhat abruptly, and Marvin is depicted in his urban environment as something of a wanderer – literally a 'stray cat' – looking for somewhere to belong.

Both *Pansy Boy* and *Reinventing Marvin* are Western narratives that navigate a visible and influential gay/LGBTQ+ culture. Turning to the Filipino film, *The Blossoming of Maximo Oliveros* (2005), we witness a similar story about an effeminate boy – a young *bakla* – trying to belong in his home and family environment, but without an identifiable Western gay or LGBTQ+ culture that Maxi can choose in favour of his physical neighbourhood. Partly for this reason, the film raises important questions about what it might mean to belong as an effeminate, same-sex attracted boy in a society that cannot easily be substituted for another and perhaps for this reason, is better able to accommodate non-conforming boys.

The Blossoming of Maximo Oliveros (hereafter *Maximo*; Filipino: *Ang Pagdadalaga ni Maximo Oliveros*) focuses on the awakening homosexuality of a gender nonconforming 12-year-old boy, Maxi, who lives in a slum in Manila, the Philippines, with his father and two adult brothers. Maxi's father ostensibly sells mobile phones for a living, but it soon becomes clear that he operates a clandestine business selling stolen goods, and that Maxi's older brothers are also implicated in the business. Nevertheless, Maxi, who is physically delicate but beautiful, is depicted as a largely happy boy who has a clear role and position in the family. With their mother dead, the Oliveros family relies upon Maxi to do traditionally female tasks. Maxi takes care of the grocery shopping, cooking, ironing, and cleaning, and we see him also take care of the younger children in the neighbourhood, ensuring that they are clean. Maxi also has a friendship network of children his own age, including other effeminate boys, with whom he participates in what some might call a drag queen show, but in the film is referred to as a 'Miss Universe' contest.

If Maxi's role in the family is clearly defined, as offering a mother-substitute presence within an otherwise strongly masculine household, he is also frequently reminded by other males that he is in many ways not like them. When we first meet Maxi, we witness his older brothers asking Maxi who he has been flirting with: he swishes his hips, wears a flower in his short hair, and is dressed in a girl's t-shirt and brightly coloured short shorts. His father and brothers joke with him about needing sanitary pads and having monthly periods. In short, Maxi's effeminate gender expression is marked and visible to other men, but it is also acceptable and is not displaced. Unlike *Reinventing Marvin*, Maxi's patriarchal household finds a place for Maxi.

The film's narrative really begins, however, when Maxi is attacked by some older adolescent boys on his way home from the Miss Universal pageant. These boys clearly know who Maxi is, and read him as being sexually available for penetration in the same way that Marvin is assumed to be penetrable by his bullies. They grab Maxi and say they want to 'see if it's smooth'; they then strip him, at which point Maxi screams 'rape!' (0:18-19). He is rescued by a new policeman, Victor, who then becomes the object of Maxi's affections. The rest of the film concentrates on Maxi's developing emotions for Victor, with clear sexual undertones, at the same time as Victor increasingly poses a threat to the Oliveros family's criminal activity. Maxi seeks to impress Victor by his female-centred interests and occupations, such as cooking and taking care of domestic chores. By this time, the wider community is aware of Maxi's involvement with Victor, and Maxi is known as the policeman's 'girl', even if the adults around him are uneasy about the inappropriate age disparity. When Victor is attacked by Maxi's brothers, to try and stop his curiosity from detecting their criminal behaviour, Maxi secretly flees to Victor's apartment to nurse him back to health. Ultimately, however, Maxi's family is torn apart by its criminal activity, and Maxi's father is killed by Victor's boss. The film ends with Maxi starting school, and living under the care of his older brothers; Victor has been distanced because of his complicity in the murder of Maxi's father.

Maximo Oliveros is a sympathetic film about a nascent *bakla* – an effeminate Filipino boy whose sexual and romantic attraction to men blossoms during the film (Garcia, 2009). Unlike Marvin Bijou, Maxi Oliveros cannot be described as marginalised or an 'exile' in his own family. He is very much at the heart of it, and his father is obviously proud of Maxi's love and affection for him and his brothers. Even though Maxi's family and neighbourhood are aware of Maxi's difference, they barely register it as being something to stigmatise, and find ways for Maxi to have a respected role in the family in ways that honour his own preferences and inclinations. They understand that Maxi is likely to be seen as a target for other men's sexual, penetrative desire, and seek to protect him from it. Maxi, on the other hand, appears to experience very little shame about the fact that he is effeminate and is attracted to older men and for this reason does not seek to displace his gender expression. The film seems more concerned with how deceit and crime destabilise a family: the death of Maxi's father is clearly meant to offer some justice, but for Maxi it represents a grievous loss that only compounds the earlier loss of his mother.

Moreover, there is little indication that Maxi will defeminise as he gets older. At the end of the film we see Maxi walk off to school dressed in school uniform but wearing a pink rucksack that his brothers indicate belongs to a girl. Even though he is seen as another male in the family, his status as a male is entirely different to that of his brothers: he is a *bakla*, and one that appears to find a sense of belonging not only in the home and family, but also in the wider community – conspicuously unlike Harfleet's pansy boy or Marvin Bijou. Maxi's effeminate mannerisms – his swishy walk, his appropriation of female clothing, his use of make-up, and his overall body language – do not seem to concern either him or others, other than that they may signal sexual availability to other men and be a target for sexual conquest.

As Western narratives, *Pansy Boy* and *Reinventing Marvin* underscore the difficulties inherent in being a gender nonconforming boy who is assumed to be same-sex attracted or may become so during adolescence. The pressure to defeminise in such spaces is strong: not only to rid oneself of effeminate mannerisms that communicate a stigmatised identity before disclosing it but to conceal any possibility that one might also be sexually available or penetrable to other men, even other gay men within an LGBTQ+ community. Feeling at risk of being defined in such ways by others, *Pansy Boy* and *Reinventing Marvin* show how protagonists use creativity and practices of re-reading themselves to take ownership of belonging to a stigmatised identity within the context of an LGBTQ+ community.

By contrast, *Maximo Oliveros* – a global majority narrative – explores the possibility of belonging as a gender nonconforming, same-sex attracted boy, without the need to extricate oneself from the place in which one grew up or to displace one's non-normative gender expression. Maxi's homosexuality – his sex object choice – is not singled out as being particularly concerning. His attraction to men, and thus his future sexual availability to men, is intricately connected to his gender expression as effeminate. This raises an interesting question as to why, in the West, sex object choice (same-sex attraction or simply 'being gay') has taken precedence over gender expression and sex role in ways that seem unnecessary in *Maximo Oliveros*. What are some of the implications of emphasising sexual orientation – being gay – over being effeminate or being a bottom? This is the question that preoccupies the next two sections of the chapter.

4.2 SEXUAL ORIENTATION AND THE TRIUMPH OF GAY

In 2021, Amazon Prime released *Everybody's Talking About Jamie* (hereafter *Jamie*), a clear successor to its 2020 film, *Dating Amber*, about a gay boy from Ireland who rejects his homophobic, provincial environment and eventually flees to London on the assurance that this is where he will be able to be his own, gay self. *Jamie*, by contrast, keeps its protagonist in the same location in which he experiences bullying – working-class Sheffield, UK. The film is based on the musical of that name, which in turn is inspired by the true story of Jamie Campbell and his desire to become a drag queen in County Durham.

And yet both *Dating Amber* and *Jamie* are problematic in their treatment of the well-trodden coming-of-age and coming-out story. *Dating Amber*, like Russell T. Davies's drama, *It's a Sin* (2021) and *Reinventing Marvin*, depict an antagonistic, polarised battle between the liberated urban metropolitan LGBTQ+ centre (which in this case is London), and backward, provincial places of misery for would-be sensitive gay males. The effect is to re-entrench perceptions of rural and suburban working-class areas as de facto spaces of marginalisation for (visibly) gay males. While *Jamie* does not make the same equivalence, the film creates a more subtle confusion, over the reasons why Jamie New is bullied in the first place.

Viewers first encounter Jamie on his 16th birthday, which in Britain, where the film is set, is, since the Sexual Offences (Amendment) Act 2000, legally the age of sexual consent for gay sex. This is significant, because while the film first introduces us to Jamie on this sexual threshold, his character is conspicuously non-sexual. This is problematic because he is ostensibly bullied because of the fact that he is gay – that he is attracted to his own sex. Jamie chooses to describe himself openly as gay, which, while reducing the amount of bullying which comes his way, still attracts some.

However, what seems most noticeable about Jamie is his effeminacy and gender nonconformity. The story positions Jamie as an archetypal *sissy boy*: effeminate, with an absent, alienated father and an over-concerned and, some might say, over-bearing mother who tries to compensate for Jamie's father's lack of interest and disappointment in his effeminate son by encouraging him – with limits – in his gender nonconforming tastes and interests. In other words, it seems obvious that Jamie is picked on at school because he is effeminate. Even though Jamie says he is gay, as do others, there is no evidence of Jamie's sex object choice, and yet the narrative uses his sex object choice – rather than his gender expression – as the reason for his marginalisation.

Ironically, it's only in his father's world of football and laddish behaviour that this is made manifest. At a key moment in the film, where Jamie has argued with his mother about her deceit in lying to him about his father's lack of interest in his desire to be a drag queen, Jamie storms off and wanders onto the football pitch at which his father's team is playing. Jamie is dressed in the team's clothes but re-styled in the form of a halter neck top and skirt. He is roughly taken off the pitch and thrown against a railing, causing his nose to bleed. His father initially defends him but then leaves him crying and bloody. The scene gestures at the truth the film is otherwise trying to conceal: that Jamie stands out because of his effeminacy, not because he is gay, and that people who target him are in fact effeminophobic rather than homophobic, although the two are of course connected. Jamie is indeed gay. It's just that we aren't permitted entrance into Jamie's sexual world, despite the film setting this up as an expectation when it starts by celebrating his 16th birthday and hence his sexual maturity. The entire film focuses on his desire to be a drag queen.

What is especially perplexing is that while the film tries so hard, and successfully, to depict the emotional life and struggles of an effeminate boy who also turns out to be gay, it cannot accurately attribute his struggles to his effeminacy – precisely what the film ostensibly wishes to bring to the foreground. Rather, the film attributes his struggles to that which is conspicuously absent – his homosexuality or same-sex attraction. *Jamie* therefore wrestles with its own premise: the spectre of effeminacy haunts Jamie, and the film admirably tries to explore his experiences, but ultimately it capitulates to the prevailing cultural narrative that gay people are often targeted – and experience non-belonging – because of their sexual orientation rather than their gender nonconformity.

Exactly the same problem is at work in the 2017 BBC documentary, *Olly Alexander: Growing Up Gay* (hereafter *Growing Up Gay*), which was commissioned as part of the BBC's efforts to mark the 50th anniversary of the partial de-criminalisation of homosexuality in England and Wales for consenting men in private, over the age of 21. In terms of genre, *Growing Up Gay* sits squarely alongside other 'coming out' narratives, such as Tom Daley's *Coming Up For Air* (2021), Adam Rippon's *Beautiful On the Outside* (2019), or Will Young's *To Be a Gay Man* (2020). However, its status as a documentary rather than, say, a written memoir, enables the narrative to be more assertive about its relationship to other key contemporary mental health issues, such as eating disorders in men, anxiety and depression, and LGBTQ+ drug culture, and to interview people with lived experience so that Alexander's struggles are narrated in solidarity with those of other LGBTQ+ young people. As such, the documentary aims for a highly sensitive and emotional treatment of the subject of growing up gay, which ostensibly is the piece's main focus. As Alexander explains in voice-over at the very beginning: 'I'm Olly Alexander, the lead singer for Years and Years and an out, gay man', the latter of which is said slowly and emphatically (0:00:13).

In many ways, Alexander's story is fairly typical of this very Western genre. Now located in London with its sophisticated provision for LGBTQ+ people and culture, viewers witness Alexander return to his provincial roots, in Coleford, Gloucestershire (Forest of Dean), to relive his difficult teenage years in the early 2000s. Frank about being bullied from ages nine until 15, he says how different he felt from others at school and 'like I was maybe a freak' (0:00: 09). Once the bullying ceased, Alexander explains that he then developed anorexia and bulimia, self-harmed, and struggled with anxiety and depression:

'Part of that was because I was ashamed of being gay', he adds (00:13:48) (see also Bartel, 2020).

Later, Alexander develops this emphasis on shame: 'the moment you realise you're different to everyone else', he says, 'that just plants the seeds of toxic pain, and it just grows and grows, and then it just gets larger and larger as you grow older, and I think that has a huge impact' (00:18:57-00:19:14). It's at this point in the narrative that Alexander begins to reach out to other self-identified LGBTQ+ youth, and to advocate for diversity role models in schools, tolerance and understanding for men who experience disordered eating, and a general 'encouragement and positivity for [young LGBTQ+ people] to be their authentic selves and be who they are. We have to do everything we can to make sure that happens' (00:57:00-00:57:25).

Growing Up Gay can be read in the way it's intended to be read: as an awareness raising effort to make lives easier for LGBTQ+ youth who are growing up gay. But the narrative suffers from some complexities that prevent it from achieving its maximum impact. Firstly, typical of such narratives in the late 2010s, it presents the struggles of all those subsumed under the LGBTQ+ alphabet as somehow synonymous, with the epithet *queer* used to do definitional work it struggles to do because of the internal differences and complexities faced by those who wish to self-identify as LGBTQ+. Secondly, and perhaps most crucially, Alexander glosses over one of the main reasons why he was bullied and marginalised at school: because he was effeminate and gender nonconforming. At one point in the documentary, he touches on this issue: he explains that at school,

> ...people would say to me that the things that I did were gay, or the clothes that I wore were gay. And they meant it in a negative way. And they told me to stop being gay. 'Stop behaving gay.' That I was a poof or a fag, you know. (00:46:57)

As I explore in Chapter 1, such labels are used primarily to stigmatise gender nonconformity, with the assumption that gender nonconformity – being effeminate – also indicates that you have, or will develop, a nonconforming sex object choice. The difficulty of *Growing Up Gay* is that the subject of effeminophobia is never tackled directly. Instead, it's Alexander's same-sex attraction that's positioned as the fault line that causes his suffering.

Other documentary narratives, such as Amazon's *Steelers: The World's First Gay Rugby Club* (2020), or even Gareth Thomas's autobiography *Proud* (2015), also broach the subject of homophobia, but from a radically different perspective that's perhaps truer to what homophobia really is: a pathological fear of same-sex attraction, desire, or behaviour. The gay men in *Steelers* do not report a gender-nonconforming childhood and they present as gender conforming or 'straight-passing' in adulthood. Olly Alexander and Jamie New do not. As Alexander admitted in an interview for the *Sun*, 'I was very effeminate as a kid' (22 June 2018). For men like those in *Steelers*, their journey to identifying as gay is radically different from the journeys made by those like Olly Alexander and Jamie New. On the one hand, masculine, 'straight-acting' gay men are seldom read as gay (i.e. *effeminate*) by others, but on the other hand, they have to engage in a constant, often exhausting process of coming out, wishing that 'being gay' wasn't synonymous in people's minds with being effeminate.

Growing Up Gay also teases viewers with suggestions that Alexander enjoys being a bottom: in one of the final scenes, make-up artists are applying gold glitter to Alexander's near-naked body, including underneath his jockstrap. Positioned on all fours (for ease of glitter application), Alexander references two classic gay bottom tropes: the jockstrap, and being in doggy-style, ready for being fucked. His glittery twink body is positioned for the viewer to imagine him being taken from behind. Alexander's gayness is therefore not only quite specific as effeminate, but it teases viewers with the implication that he also enjoys getting fucked.

Ultimately, of course, effeminophobia and homophobia are intimately connected, but they are not the same thing, and for those gay men who do not experience bullying because of gender nonconformity, it can be confusing to attribute effeminate boys' bullying to simply being gay and it homogenises gayness in ways that obscure its diversity There are different kinds of gay male. *Growing Up Gay* only narrates one kind of gay: it tells of the experience and struggles of an effeminate gay male who experiences both effeminophobia and homophobia and may enjoy bottoming too. The documentary would have been more compelling had it openly admitted this, and sought to raise awareness of how gender nonconforming experience can, for some boys and men, intersect with being gay, and how this double stigmatisation causes specific problems that require specific responses – in schools, for example, where the search for belonging is key (see Chapter 2). As Glick et al. maintain: 'attitudes are more negative toward the "doubly deviant" [Effeminate Gay Man] than toward the [Masculine Gay Man] type' (2007, p. 55). Instead, like *Jamie*, *Growing Up Gay* narrates the triumph of gay: gender expression and sex roles become of secondary importance in understanding social attitudes and behaviours to the detriment, ironically, of fully understanding the many ways that one can be gay. Indeed, not only are the experiences of males like Olly Alexander and Jamie New misinterpreted; those of very different kinds of gay men are also misinterpreted.

By contrast, the Spanish documentary *Samantha Hudson* (2018) (hereafter *Samantha*) refuses to subordinate gender expression and sex roles from an analysis of a young gay man's experience. Iván Gonzalez Ranedo, who is often known by his drag queen persona, 'Samantha Hudson', is presented not only as gay, but as an effeminate bottom, which is mirrored in promotional photos. His experiences only make sense by reference to all three aspects of himself, which the documentary explores. And as a documentary in the gay *bildungsroman* genre, it is more sophisticated and nuanced than *Growing Up Gay*. *Samantha* succeeds where Alexander's fails because it is unafraid to explore the specifics of Hudson's experience as an effeminate young gay man who openly labels himself as a bottom, or to be more precise, as a power bottom, emphasising his assertive enjoyment in taking cock.

The documentary opens by exploring the origins of Hudson's well-known 2015 song, 'Soy maricón' (trans. *I'm a faggot*), which directly infers that Hudson identifies with a traditional Spanish identity which links together sex object choice, gender expression, and sex role as a *pasivo*. The documentary's main conceit is to show how Hudson develops as a self-identified *maricón* through the use of social media such as Instagram – one who is comfortable with his gender nonconformity and is candid about his sexual life as a power bottom. Like Alexander, Hudson flees from his provincial home (in Majorca) to the metropolitan opportunities that Barcelona presents for LGBTQ+ people. Here he is able to 'come out' as Samantha: a gay oriented male who combines feminine and masculine traits. Throughout the film, Hudson is depicted as embodied in his male body, but driven towards exaggeratedly female dress and behaviour. He frequently uses the word *loca* or *loco* (meaning 'crazy') to describe himself, with obvious overtones to the way in which *loca* describes overtly effeminate homosexual males in Latin contexts – cross-dressing *pasivos* who imitate 'whores' rather than an 'average woman'.

Arriving at this synthesis of maleness and femininity, Hudson explains:

> *Iván and Samantha are not like two different things. I mean, when I was a kid, I thought I was trans. So, to explore all these things, I created a drag-queen character called Giovanna Bon Dage. And I made a separation [separación], a dichotomy, between my masculine self that was Iván, and my feminine self that was Giovanna Bon Dage. So, I was like differentiating my personality in two ways. Later, I realized that was absurd, because I didn't have to separate myself into two, it's completely understandable that in the same person there is a feminine side and a masculine side. So, Samantha would be like the representation of this thought or this*

reflection that I became aware. So, for me, Samantha is like Iván and Giovanna together [juntos], like an evolution of myself. And that's what I am now. It's like the combination of those two personalities I thought I had to separate [separar]. (00:08:03-00:09:15)

Hudson's autobiographical narrative is consistent with the scholarly understanding that gender nonconforming gay men very likely had gender nonconforming boyhoods, and that they were often bullied as such by others. Like Alexander, Hudson was also taunted by other children at school. But unlike Alexander, Hudson attributes this specifically to the fact that he was read as effeminate. In an interview with Spanish magazine El Español, Hudson explains that when he was younger he was called *mariquita*, which specifically denotes a *sissy boy*, or, as might be said in the US, someone *faggy* (Galeano, 2022; Maldonado, 2021). For Hudson, his attraction to men is inextricably connected to his gender nonconformity and his sense of non-belonging as a typical male in his society. *Samantha* tells the story of his struggle with feeling different, and how his alter ego 'Samantha Hudson' is a way for him to belong with these different aspects of himself in his body.

Moreover, unlike *Growing Up Gay*, *Samantha* is remarkably honest about Hudson's sexuality as a power bottom (see Brennan, 2016a). When touring his bedroom, Hudson picks up a large dildo and explains that, while he has only used it once, it still sits pride of place on his shelf – a scene which is replicated in a promotional image for the Spanish online magazine, Vein. His body is very much on the twinky side, emphasising his physical vulnerability to the men he talks about submitting to sexually, even as he seeks to dominate their cocks and ingest their semen. In one of his Instagram videos, which is replayed in the documentary, Hudson talks explicitly about his struggle as a bottom:

I've had a lot of anal sex. Like a table leg was beating up my ass. And I've realised that I don't like it. I mean, I like it because I enjoy it, but it doesn't satisfy me. The more I do it, the less I feel like I want to repeat. I wish I was a sex hooligan [hooligan de sexo]. I wish I was a super fan and said 'Hey, sex, I love you'. But I can't. It's so hard. Unless it's with your husband. (00:24:07-00:24:36)

Responding to a fan's suggestion that he stops being a *pasivo* or a bottom, he says emphatically that he would not do that: 'The conflict is not in the role I adopt in bed, because I'm very happy to be a power bottom [*power bottom*], it's just that it's so hard for me to create a link with a person' (00:27:02-00:27:10). Hudson uses the documentary to invite intimacy concerning his sex life, which is bound up with this artistic project of 'Samantha Hudson', which in turn arises out of his earlier struggle to belong with his effeminacy and sexual attraction to men.

A key difference that might explain why two Western narratives - *Growing Up Gay* and *Samantha* – offer very different interpretations and depictions of the lives of effeminate gay men is that Olly Alexander is relatively well-known, and his documentary was for the BBC to mark an event specifically related to remembering the partial decriminalisation of homosexuality in England and Wales, whereas Samantha Hudson is little known outside the Spanish context, and cultivates a much less clean-cut image than Alexander and attracts social media followers for precisely that reason.

Nevertheless, these differences notwithstanding, *Samantha* is intellectually and artistically more rewarding as a documentary. It deliberately attempts to analyse the relationship between sex object choice and gender expression, and is candid about the role of sexuality in mediating and expressing these. While the documentary does not attempt to hide Hudson's homosexuality (he talks frequently about sexual liaisons with other men), it does not put 'being gay' on a pedestal when it comes to the lived experiences of effeminate gay males.

Effeminacy, and the challenges this causes in terms of belonging, is very much foregrounded as well. It's possible that Hudson's access to traditional Latin labels such as *maricón*, and the worldviews associated with gender stratified or heterogendered forms of homosexuality (see Chapter 1), mean that Hudson has more cultural capital to draw on in consolidating his own identity than does Alexander or even Jamie New. Even though Alexander notes being called a *poof* at school, it's hard to imagine him creating a song entitled 'I'm a poof' that would strike quite the same cultural resonance as Hudson's 'Soy maricón', or, as I shall show, as the Brazilian term *poc*. Although, of course, it could be said that this is precisely what Paul Harfleet is attempting to do, albeit for younger children, through the Pansy Project and his invocation of the *pansy boy*.

4.3 BOTTOM AS A DISPOSABLE AND DETACHABLE LABEL

Samantha Hudson also draws attention to the way in which *bottom* as identity and *bottoming* as sexual activity have become politicised and in some cases opposed as radically different attitudes to Western gay life. Increasingly, *bottoming* is the preferred term to describe insertee sexual behaviour among men as opposed to *bottom*, which some fear perpetuates heteronormative stereotypes and boxes gay men into a submissive, sexually unadventurous role. Writing for Xtra Magazine, writer Alex Green has argued that,

> *Topping or bottoming (or being vers for that matter) is not an identity; it's a thing you do until it's done [...] a person is more than their preferred position, and that position tells you much less than you think about who they are and their social worlds.* (2020, n.p.)

In other words, Green wishes to move beyond speaking about tops and bottoms as categories of gay men, principally because they appear to inscribe heteronormative roles which Green believes are limiting and oppressive. Green notes that 'freeing oneself from those gendered expectations and assumptions opens up space to explore desires, sensations and relations that might otherwise be foreclosed'.

This is all well and good for those who do feel that being considered a top or a bottom is a limiting identity to assume. But such an argument seems unconscious of the way in which its very Western and LGBTQ+-centric politics – which looks askance at what it considers heteronormative – flattens those identities that very much align with the bottom or top as kinds of persons, rather than a sheer activity (McGill & Collins, 2015). This was one of the major reasons why the subreddit r/TopsAndBottoms was established, to provide a space for self-identified tops and bottoms to belong where they were not pressured into adopting a versatile sexual politics in which tops and bottoms became verbs, and thus no longer different kinds of people (Vytniorgu, 2024a).

The antagonism towards bottoms as a distinct category of gay men is also prevalent in paratexts around gay porn. For example, one of the most vocal of pro-versatile users commenting on gay porn on the porn sharing website, myvidster.com, refers to bottoms as 'onesided [*sic*] queens', and observes that,

> *To this day there are folk that still conceive of being gay as being simply a shitty copy-paste version of straight folk, where one of the two is a female substitute that gets emasculated and whose dick is but a vestigial organ, while the other is a deranged 'straight' male that can't find pussy so he settles for an ass.*

For this commentator, Daddy/twink dynamics, or any heterogender pairing in which there is a contrasting gendered element to the eroticism, is roundly condemned. In one video for RawStrokes featuring models Marco Paris (top Daddy) and Daniel Hausser (bottom twink), this user writes 'if you ever wondered what you would get if you crossbred a broom with a poodle, then here you have it. I bet you could swipe the floor with that effeminate queen's hairdo'. Here, this user rejects Hausser as an 'effeminate queen', equating his consistent role as a bottom to more masculine tops as a form of identity that is not only undesirable (in the eyes of this user) because Hausser's penis is merely 'vestigial', but also has historical precedent and one that this user would gladly see consigned to the dustbin of gay queen history. Not everyone shares these acerbic opinions, and even in this one video, another user writes: 'bro, no one fucking cares about your stupid thoughts about fem gays and bottoms [...] get a fucking life and stop hating on other people's preferences'.

At the complete opposite end of the spectrum, one Tumblr user has argued that,

> ...bottom is both a 'gender' and a 'sexual orientation.' It's a comprehensive identity and way of life, based on embracing one's natural femininity and receptivity, one's inferiority to and complementarity to Men. A true bottom turns her receptivity according to nature into freely-chosen and actualised complete acceptance.

For this blogger, being a bottom is, as they say, a 'comprehensive identity and way of life'; it is much more than an activity that one does and then gets over with, as Green would argue. A model like Hausser, for instance, would in this scheme of things be understandable as an effeminate bottom who is simply playing to what is 'natural' for them. Even if he is labelled a *queen*, it would not be done so in a disparaging way, but rather recognising that his status as a *fem bottom* is internally coherent, synthesising sex object choice (attraction to masculine Daddies), gender expression (as feminine or effeminate), and sex role (as a bottom) and at the same time distinguishing him quite clearly from the men he has sex with, capitalised as Men.

Outside the world of porn and erotica, which I shall turn to in more detail in Chapter 5, it remains the case that finding a *via media* between, on the one hand, dismissing *bottom* as an identity altogether, and on the other hand, calling it an entire gender and sexual orientation, is difficult, and as such, has implications for belonging. The Australian-South African singer-song writer Troye Sivan has courted speculation about his status as a bottom, and openly identifies as effeminate, even though he is still uneasy about his gender nonconformity.

The case of Sivan represents a relatively mainstream openly gay singer-actor navigating the waters of bottoms and bottoming. Is he a bottom, or does he merely sing about bottoming? To what extent can he be claimed as a bottom icon? For Sivan, the answer is quite categorical: 'completely reductive', he stated in a 2018 interview for them. magazine (Davis, 2018, n.p.). And yet despite Sivan's reluctance to be specific about his sex roles in bed, his 2018 song 'Bloom' has generally been interpreted to be about bottoming, launching the Twitter/X hashtag #BopsBoutBottoming, which Sivan himself Tweeted (since deleted). Rhetoric scholar Cory Geraths has read 'Bloom' in the context of *anthos*, which uses 'floral metaphors to describe attractive young men' and is also a metaphor for bottoming (2022, p. 258). Geraths recognises that 'for many gay men "bottom" denotes not only a sexual act but also an identity with particular codes, behaviors, and expectations' (p. 259). 'Bloom' therefore invites readings and identifications with bottom personae as well as the act of bottoming.

Moreover, Sivan is also repeatedly categorised as a twink, as Geraths acknowledges. Writing for i-D Magazine, Brian O'Flynn has shown how 'twinky role models like Olly Alexander and Troye Sivan, who have come forward in recent years and celebrated their femininity, are doing positive work reducing the stigma of femmephobia' (2018, n.p.). My reservations about Alexander aside, Sivan has been more explicit about connecting his reputation as a fem twink to #BopsBoutBottoming. In 2021, Sivan released an additional music video entitled 'Angel Baby', which depicts Sivan on a motorbike, topless, and with the top of his black thong showing. Not only is Sivan positioned in this video as in some way feminised or effeminate, he also pairs himself with a more obviously masculine man who drives the motorbike assertively into the distance, with Sivan clinging to him, his slim arms contrasting his partner's muscular ones. In his more recent music video, 'Rush' (2023), the focus on bottoms is intensified dramatically through frames focusing on male bottoms in jockstraps – a quintessentially gay item of clothing designed to draw attention to the bottom as a male sexual site. As with Olly Alexander who allowed himself to be filmed wearing a jockstrap, Sivan adopts a similar cultural object to communicate his sexual aim, as opposed simply to his sexual object.

It's scenes such as these, in addition to Sivan's coy evasions about his status as a bottom, that provoke viewer responses like those found in a Data Lounge thread from 2018 after 'Bloom' was released, entitled 'Troye Sivan: "labelling me as a bottom is reductive"'. Here, online users respond to Sivan's self-presentation with comments such as 'does she really think we're going to buy her as anything but a bottom? Gurl, please' (R1); 'Self-hating bottom' (R14); and 'This gurl ain't never topped anyone in her LIFE!!' (R21). While these somewhat tongue-in-cheek comments are intended to highlight a paradox facing gay viewers who follow Sivan's music and evaluate his style in light of his own comments about himself, they also resonate with Sivan's own ambiguous and conflicted attitude towards his gender nonconformity.

Unlike Olly Alexander, Troye Sivan is quite open in media interviews about the way in which his effeminacy has impacted him in complex ways. In a 2018 interview for the *Guardian*, for example, he confessed: 'I have to get comfortable with the fact that I am kind of effeminate sometimes – or really effeminate sometimes [...] That I want to paint my nails. Overcoming all those stupid rules that society embeds in you as a kid about gender and sexuality is a conscious task' (Snapes, 2019). Producing songs about bottoming, and using effeminate markers such as a thong and jockstrap, in addition to the more subtle flower imagery that Geraths has read as 'Bloom's' queer rhetoric – *anthos* – means that Sivan is, at least to some degree, attempting to wrestle with what it means to have a bottom identity, to be gender nonconforming, and to be openly gay, belonging with all three aspects of himself.

In short, Sivan is publicly contemplating a role for himself as a fem gay bottom, even though this is heavily qualified by statements implying that he has no such fixed identity. The fact that Sivan does qualify them also has implications for gay or LGBTQ+ audiences who are ready to identify or belong with an openly fem gay bottom, but who feel frustrated that they cannot do so because Sivan himself is still reluctant to conflate all three as being integral to himself.

As this chapter has already shown, Sivan is navigating a very specific Western context in which the detaching of sexual orientation (sex object choice) from questions of gender expression and anal sex role (sexual aim) is prevalent and often policed by those who are queasy about any conflation of being gay with gender nonconformity and taking a receptive role in anal sex. By contrast, when one moves outside the Western LGBTQ+ context, more diverse representations can occur.

In the rest of this chapter, I will briefly discuss the music of contemporary Brazilian singer and songwriter Gabeu, who is boldly claiming a space for rural gay effeminacy in Brazil by explicitly drawing attention to the effeminate bottom. I will then explore some representations of Indian *kothis*, who publicly negotiate precisely the combination of stigmatised identities that Sivan skirts around and other narratives such as those explored above avoid highlighting.

Gabeu (Gabriel Silva Felizardo, born 1998) is a Brazilian singer and songwriter who has garnered attention for his commitment to raising the profile of rural LGBTQ+ singers and country music in Brazil, under the term *queernejo*, which is a queer reworking of the traditional, heteronormative genre of *sertanejo* (Galvão, 2022); Gabeu's (2021) album, which includes the single 'Amor Rural' (released 2019), is entitled AGROPOC, bringing together the rural with *poc* – a Brazilian slang term for an effeminate gay male, presumed to be a *passivo* or a bottom.

Gabeu's public persona is reminiscent of Hudson's, although without the cross-dressing and an alternative female drag persona. Rather, Gabeu is able to draw on the Brazilian cultural label and imagery of *poc*, with its own cultural associations specifically tied to effeminacy and bottom identity. His innovation, however, is to place the *poc* in the space of the countryside, which is traditionally considered masculine and unwelcome to LGBTQ+ people. 'Amor Rural' is defiant about taking up space in the countryside for those who are not expected to do so: 'vamo assumir o nosso amor rural' ['let's declare our rural love']. While both Gabeu and Marvin Bijou recognise the effeminophobia and homophobia of rural spaces, Gabeu rejects the notion that LGBTQ+ people only belong in urban spaces, and instead chooses to queer rural creative genres, such as *sertanejo*, in order to claim a space in which *pocs* like him can belong. Gabeu uses one Brazilian cultural trope – the *sertanejo* – to create space for another – the *poc*. And the *poc* explicitly welcomes synergies between gender nonconformity and bottom identity in ways resisted by figures such as Sivan and Alexander. In India, the term *kothi* does similar cultural work, although as I shall show, is increasingly viewed with suspicion by those interested in more Western, LGBTQ+ identities.

Scholars have variously defined *kothis* as 'natal male androphiles who primarily take the receptive role in anal sex with men and are gender atypical to some degree' (Stief, 2017, p. 75); they 'are not only characterized by passive roles in anal sex but by a sense of self premised on feminine sensibility that in some circumstances may involve wearing female clothing and make-up' (Boyce, 2007, p. 178); '*kothis* are those men who "like to do women's work" and desire the passive/receptive position in same-sex encounters with other men' (Reddy, 2001, p. 95); and is a term 'used by many effeminate men to signal their preference for being receptive (bottom) partners during sexual intercourse among men who have sex with men' (Gill, 2016, p. 1).

In short, scholars broadly agree that, as Stief argues, *kothi* is defined in terms 'of a combination of sexual attraction, position preference in anal sex (insertive/receptive), and gender presentation', and that *kothi* is different to *hijra*, which tends to be conceptualised as a transgendered identity (2017, p. 82). A 2018 study by Cecilia Tomori and colleagues elicited some autobiographical narratives from *kothis* that stress the core experience of having an adult male body but being sexually attracted to men and having a feminine gendered subjectivity. One *kothi*, aged 20, noted that 'I am *kothi* because all my activities are like that of [a] female. I have feminine nature' (p. 238).

Another, aged 40, noted that 'from my childhood I am attracted toward male people that are the same gender' (p. 238).

These narratives echo those in the 2010 documentary, *Being Male, Being Kothi*, directed by Mahuya Bandyopadhyay, for the Public Service Broadcasting Trust. Set in Kolkata, the documentary follows the day-to-day lives of several *kothis* as they prepare for a Pride March, thereby underscoring the tensions at play with Westernised middle-class gay identities and political activism. The documentary makes it clear that *kothis* disagree about what the term actually means, and some object to its association with being passive in anal sex with men or being an explicitly feminine identity. Other *kothis*, such as Biton, affirm these characteristics, which accord with the scholarly literature.

Those who speak the most in the documentary have at least some facility in English, which also perhaps explains why it's these speakers, rather than those who do not speak English, who demonstrate familiarity with Westernised concepts around rights and 'prevalent social gender constructs' and are also hesitant about conflating gender nonconformity and sexual receptivity (00:19: 18). During the March, viewers see images of local men, presumed to be *kothis*, holding banners with messages in English such as 'Homosexuality is our Birth Right' and 'Stop Discrimination on basis of Gender, Sexuality, or Disability'.

The political mobilisation of *kothis* in the documentary is tied to an explicit awareness of HIV, and as Paul Boyce has noted, it is through Western-centric HIV prevention initiatives that identities such as *kothi* have come to the fore and often contrasted with the gay identity that is taken up by more middle-class Indians and those who perhaps find *kothi* identities too restrictive. But as Boyce (2007) also admits, the conceptualisation of *kothi* is itself imbricated with HIV prevention strategies, often taking its 'indigenous' status at face value while overlooking how this so-called 'subjectivity' has been constructed through HIV prevention strategies that position the *kothi* as an at-risk group. In short, *kothi* is a contested term that is increasingly being conceptualised in the context of Western gay understandings of sexual and gender possibility, but it is a contest that is being played out publicly.

Kothi therefore remains a pertinent identity synergising gender expression, sex object choice and sex role, even though in private these might be more mixed than the *effeminate bottom* narrative might initially suggest. In her sensitive photographs of *kothis* in Tamil Nadu, journalist Candace Feit has highlighted the performative dimension of *kothi* sensibility while also emphasising the continued struggles faced by *kothis* who may, under social pressure, be married with children. As she noted in an interview for The Morning News in 2014:

> *I wanted to get a deeper understanding of how some of the people I met lived their daily lives and navigated expected roles within their families and the broader community – especially since I knew that several of the kothis I had met were married and had children, or were being pressured by their families to do so.*
>
> (Rabarison, 2014, n.p.)

A Woman in My Heart (2015) echoes *Being Male, Being Kothi* in its celebration of *kothi* belonging: these are gender nonconforming, largely same-sex attracted males who build community together through gender nonconforming communal practices. A large percentage of the images in the collection focus on intimate practices of care, such as applying make-up, brushing hair or preparing food.

Images such as 'Dinesha carries water into the temple in Devanipattinam. September 2014' (Fig. 1) focus on the effeminate gender presentation among *kothis*. This image in particular echoes Biton's narrative in *Being Male, Being Kothi*: 'as I was growing up, if I wore a sari or churidar I felt shy. I would go to school and the effeminacy was still there in me...would sway my hips and walk' (00:04:25-00:08:45). The *kothis* in *A Woman in My Heart* highlight their gender nonconformity through dress, mannerisms, and traditional 'women's activities'. Feit's focus on detail is also explained in part by her decision to use film: 'I think shooting in film helps a lot. It forces me to compose more deliberately [...] Working slowly is my attempt to combat the willful stupidity with some thoughtfulness' (Rabarison, 2014, n.p.). For Feit, this thoughtfulness is necessary to tell accurate stories about people who face considerable challenges, describing her work as a form of activism: 'My goal with my work is to connect with people and try to tell their stories in a human way. Through these connections and stories, something – attitudes, behaviors – might slowly shift' (Rabarison, 2014, n.p.).

As with Paul Harfleet's *Pansy Boy*, Gabeu's 'Amor Rural' or Marvin Bijou's play in *Reinventing Marvin*, Feit's *A Woman in My Heart* turns to creativity and storytelling to highlight the challenges faced by those on the margins. While bottom identity is not the main focus of Feit's work, it is nevertheless present in *Being Male, Being Kothi*, and demonstrates the way in which non-gay identities outside the West are utilised to conceptualise a felt sense of difference: in this case, desiring other men, being gender nonconforming, and preferring receptive anal sex with masculine male partners.

While Boyce may be sceptical about the way in which *kothi* has been assimilated to HIV prevention programmes and perhaps misread as a traditional indigenous identity, conversely, could it not also be the case that

Fig. 1. Dinesha Carries Water Into the Temple in Devanipattinam. September 2014 (Feit, 2015).

regardless of its fairly recent surge in popularity, the term has enabled a certain group of males to be able to speak about their desire and identity in new ways? This is precisely the manner in which Matthew Stief (2017) has recently written about *kothis*. And, as Rictor Norton (2016) has emphasised in his historical work on effeminacy and homosexuality in the West, it is not necessary that something be labelled for it to be true or for it to exist.

A key difference, therefore, between the image of Dinesha and the depiction of Sivan riding the motorbike with his thong showing is that Dinesha's identity as a *kothi* already enables him, at least in part, to balance different aspects of his gender and sexuality: his cocked hip and swaying arm, combined with his 'women's work' of carrying water, publicly communicate who he is in a meaningful way. For Sivan, as he noted in his interview for the *Guardian*, it is an ongoing struggle to reconcile his effeminacy, his negotiation of bottoming and 'reductive' bottom identity, and his status as an openly gay singer/actor.

Contemporary Western narratives tend to marginalise fem gay bottoms in three main ways: (1) by overlooking the significance of effeminophobia – rather than homophobia – in some gay men's experience and thereby decentring effeminacy in their lives and the spaces in which they display this, (2) by emphasising the centrality of sexual orientation (sex object choice) over gender expression and anal sex role (sexual aim) and (3) by preferring to think of bottom as a verb that one does rather than a noun that one is and can be enacted in different places and spaces. When these three phenomena are experienced together, a state of marginalisation within LGBTQ+ communities and politics can ensue, with an attendant search for belonging as a fem gay bottom.

In the next chapter, I explore some of the ways in which Western fem bottoms seek to belong in practice, primarily through online erotic and pornographic fantasy spaces, which, while transcending geographical and cultural borders in ways that the narratives in this chapter do not, nevertheless still reveal significant cultural fault lines between Western and non-Western representations of effeminacy and bottom identities and performances.

5

FEM BOTTOMS IN PRACTICE

This chapter focuses specifically and extensively on the ways in which fem bottoms consolidate their identities and how others respond to those who refuse to subordinate their gender nonconformity and preference for bottoming to their sexual orientation, as detailed in the previous chapter. I explore narratives by and about Western gay males who, like some of the *kothis* explored in Chapter 4, insist on the mutually reinforcing relationship between being fem, a bottom and partnering with masculine top men. The chapter explores a range of sexual fantasy narratives which illuminate the contours of sexual preference and desire in ways that analysing actual behaviour might obscure (Moskowitz & Garcia, 2019; Swift-Gallant et al., 2021). In doing so, this chapter positions sexual fantasy as a creative way to consolidate and explore marginalised sex role preferences.

5.1 THE FEM BOTTOM MODEL

Far from being a peripheral feature of gay men's lives, porn is central to the gay imagination in the West (Mercer, 2017). Gay men often learn about being gay and having gay sex through watching porn, and the accessibility of gay porn on social media and smartphones has increased its variety, quantity and accessibility (Mowlabocus, 2010). However, there are ways in which gay men who consume porn police the kind of porn that gets produced and which is subsequently consumed by other men (and some women, of course). One of the ways in which this happens is by openly criticising effeminate models, even if they are bottoms. While twink porn is a recognised and established genre of gay porn and twinks are not expected to be especially masculine, there nevertheless seems to be a line that is drawn. They cannot be *too* fem.

The American model Bar Addison is one such fem bottom who has come under scrutiny for being too fem. Addison is a white, relatively slim, handsome model who would more accurately fit the description of *twunk* – a hybrid between a *twink* and a *hunk*, although he is frequently described as a twink. He has a lightly muscular body with little obvious body fat. Professionally, he has worked for studios such as FamilyDick, Lucas Entertainment, Next Door Twink and Southern Strokes. Sexually, he is primarily a bottom, although more recently he has topped. But in viewers' imaginations, he seems to be typecast as a bottom. While Addison's case is especially pronounced, there are similar derogatory comments following videos featuring other white American fem bottom models such as Tannor Reed, Leo Grand and Ryan Evans.

However, Addison is distinctive among contemporary Western gay erotic models because his effeminacy is noted and commented on elaborately by viewers and commentators in uploaded videos to sharing platforms such as XVideos, XHamster or BoyfriendTV. One blogger has described Addison as 'such a twinky twink', whose 'slight body and effeminate mannerisms' contribute to his 'twinky-ness'. There are also occasional positive comments from viewers. One viewer on XVideos wrote how glad he was to 'stumble upon the very cute & sexy Bar Addison. His fem way of speaking contradicts his muscular, gorgeous body [...] He's such an instant stiff with that perfect body and vulnerable sounding manner of speaking'. Another viewer has suggested that 'Bar's voice is really sweet'.

But the vast majority of comments are negative. A sample selection of 32 videos available online featuring Addison divulges the following descriptors used to categorise Addison as an effeminate bottom: 'faggy bottom'; 'total fag'; 'queen'; 'girly-boy'; 'girly twink'; 'camp sissy'; 'mincing machine'; 'nellie'; 'femboy'; 'whining pussy' and 'nellie queen'. Nearly all are written in a derogatory tone, deliberately trying to discredit Addison's status as a legitimate porn model.

Addison's effeminacy as a bottom seems to ruin any scene in which he stars. One user writes that 'this entire scene, like so many, is ruined by the casting of Bar Addison [...] Could he *be* anymore camp?' Another writes that 'the camp sissy ruins the video'. Some users suggest that whoever is paired with Addison would be better off with someone more masculine: 'Can they not get some twink who is not so fucking effeminate?' asked one user. 'It would have been better and hotter with a less effeminate boy', wrote another. Another cries: 'The twink is such a queen, UGH! The grandfather is hot but he really needs to fuck a man'.

Together, these comments highlight the perceived incongruity between Addison's body and his voice, which is taken as a proxy for his overall gender expression as effeminate. The fact that he is cast as a twink bottom is not in itself a problem for these viewers. What matters is his effeminacy, and the comments directed against this are best interpreted as effeminophobic rather than strictly homophobic. A comment such as 'hot body, but awful voice', or 'Bar is smoking hot ... as long as he doesn't talk', speak of non-belonging. The idea of effeminate belonging for Addison is excluded in part because effeminacy is not supposed to reside in someone who, unless he opens his mouth, is considered 'hot' because he looks masculine. As explored in Chapters 2 and 3, this is also an issue of perceived mismatch between body and gender expression, which may in part be influenced by psychobiological factors beyond someone's control. A model with Addison's relatively masculine body should not, by this logic, be so effeminate.

Anything that might indicate gender nonconformity is rigidly policed by viewers. One viewer argues decisively that 'masc dudes are the way to go. Hot as fuck. Get all these faggy ass fairy fem bottoms out of here'. Words such as *faggy*, *fairy*, *nelly* or *queen* have a long lineage in American discourse to refer specifically to males who embody a combination of homosexuality, effeminacy and being sexually passive/receptive that has been heavily resisted by other gay men since the Second World War (see Chapter 2). These are words that at one time denoted a more or less cohesive type that has since been largely discarded and discredited wherever possible as damaging to gay men's quest for acceptance as masculine men whose only distinctive characteristic is their sexual orientation or sex object choice – their attraction to other men (Houlbrook, 2005). One viewer lays out such a philosophy in acerbic detail: bottoms are 'pitiful' because,

> *I'm into men, you know, the whole point of homosexuality is same-sex attraction. If I want to fuck an effeminate emasculated creature that lacks a functional dick, I'll fuck females. Secondly, I like gay porn, you know, porn that involves two or more men and not some pitiful mockery of a straight flick, where one of the guys is the glorified 'man' while the other is a female substitute.*

It should be said that this viewer's comments are often criticised by other viewers, who think they are too extreme. But some agree with him.

What this comment represents, however, is the way in which an extreme version of 'masc4masc' – masculine men having sex with other masculine men – has permeated American gay culture to the point where being gay itself is synonymous with a masculinist vision of homosexuality which is reducible to an issue of sex object choice (Sarson, 2020). Models such as Bar Addison, Ryan Evans, Leo Grand, Tannor Reed or Dallas Preston, who are white American males, are criticised for failing to live up to this way of being gay. In one of his videos, Reed himself has been read as an 'effeminate broken third wheel', cramping the style of masculine men with functional dicks. Evans, similarly, is discredited in one of his videos by being read as 'a limp wristed, campy, vampy, eye rolling, slapped up, nellie queen, fem boy', who, in another video, 'couldn't be butch if his life depended on it'.

While comments about white American or northern European porn models are often negative if effeminacy is perceived, even in a twink bottom, comments about models in a Latin American context are somewhat more lenient, which raises questions about the reasons for tolerating an effeminate bottom in a Latin context and not in a white American one. Building on the pioneering work of Joseph Carrier, ethnographers such as Stephen Murray (1995), Manuel Fernández-Alemany and Murray (2002), Héctor Carrillo (2002, 2014), Richard Parker (1999), Don Kulick (1998) and Annick Prieur (1998) have been instrumental over the past 25 years in detailing the sexual dynamics of Latin American men who have sex with men, where there now often exists a hybridity between so-called traditional forms of heterogender homosexuality and modern, American 'gay' notions. The former denotes a coupling of a *macho* who is defined by his masculinity and status as a penetrator, and a *pasivo*, who is defined by his effeminacy and readiness to be penetrated – orally and anally – by 'real men'.

As these scholars insist, this is often more a *pasivo* sexual fantasy and ideal type than a true record of people's actual behaviour, and *pasivos* can be quick to police their partner's masculinity: any hint of being a possible *pasivo* like them and a *macho* is rejected (Fernández-Alemany & Murray, 2002, pp. 78–81; Murray, 2000, p. 268). By contrast, *gay* refers to a more 'egalitarian' situation in which masculine, homosexually identified men seek each other as sexual partners and may adopt a more versatile sexual repertoire in bed, depending on the given partner. However, as Fernández-Alemany and Murray explain, *gay* can simply constitute a new word to refer to an old phenomenon (*gay* = effeminate *pasivo*), or it could be something genuinely hybrid (2002, pp. 8–9; Carrillo, 1999).

Videos uploaded to porn hosting sites such as XVideos and XHamster attract numerous comments from viewers located in Central and South America, and the language they use to describe the models in these videos reflects the tensions of a hybrid traditional-modern understanding of male homosexuality that scholars have analysed at length outside the world of porn. What is fascinating, however, is that in the realm of sexual fantasy, traditional heterogender pairings of a *macho* and *pasivo* are prolific, and effeminate bottoms are often accepted as natural.

For example, Ariano is a model who has worked for the American studios FamilyDick and Latin Leche and is, to the best of my knowledge, Argentinian. As a fem bottom, his performance is not vastly different to fellow fem bottom Ryan Evans, who has also worked for FamilyDick, but who is often criticised for being too fem as a white American male. By contrast, Ariano's status as a fem bottom is praised by viewers. One viewer argues that 'the Latin bottom is cute and hot, but needs to moan more and be more expressive'. Where Bar Addison is derided for having a fem voice and moaning, Ariano is encouraged to moan more and seems to belong as a 'little bitch'. Other viewers have referred to him positively as a 'submissive boy' and a 'fag'. Only one viewer I came across suggested that Ariano is too effeminate: 'It's a pity the bottom young guy speaks like a woman (I hate that), because he looks nice, but his voice is terribly effeminate'.

By contrast, Spanish and Portuguese speakers commenting on Ariano's videos have little difficulty accepting his status as an effeminate *pasivo*. One refers to him as a *loquita* – a diminutive version of *loca*, used as a proxy for effeminate bottom or *queen* (literally 'crazy woman'), and which is also used in the same video to refer to Ariano. The video in question sets up a narrative where Ariano is a heterosexual young man who sucks cock and gets fucked in order to earn some money for his girlfriend (Fig. 2).

Spanish and Portuguese-speaking viewers find this incredulous: 'A este chico le encanta la verga, como habla, su forma de vestir, sus greñas, sus cejas delineadas, está rico pero de hetero no tiene ni brizna [This boy loves cock: how

Fig. 2. Screenshot of Ariano in 'Numero 28' (Latin Leche/Say Uncle, 2018).

he talks, his clothes, his floppy hair, his defined eyebrows – he's hot but doesn't have an ounce of hetero in him]'.[1] Another argues: 'Si quieren hacer creer que el pasivo no es gay por lo menos busquen un pasivo serio pues este de hetero no tiene ni la voz [If you want us to believe that this bottom isn't gay then at least look for a serious bottom because this "hetero" doesn't even have the voice]'. Other Spanish and Portuguese-speaking commentators in the same video refer to Ariano as a *florecita* ('little flower') a *mariquita* ('sissy') with a 'pinta de marica* [look of a fairy]', and a *superpasiva* ('uber bottom'), the latter written in the feminine to emphasise the mutually reinforcing components of Ariano's effeminacy and his status as a bottom who sucks cock and gets fucked.

As a Latin American model who is predominantly cast as a fem bottom, Ariano is one of a number of other bottoms from Latin American contexts in which their status as an effeminate bottom is largely celebrated rather than reviled by viewers, especially Spanish and Portuguese speakers who comment on their videos. For example, the Argentinian model 'Fox', who has worked for Schoolboy Secrets, is declared to be a 'perfect bottom', an 'adorable bottom', a *marica* and *mariquita* [*fairy* and *sissy*] and a *putita* [*whore*]. Nicolas, another Argentinian who models for Schoolboy Secrets (among other studios), is referred to as a 'perfect little sissy twink', a 'cute boy [who] sounds like a girl with that big cock in his ass', a 'nice pussyboy', a 'feminine bottom', a 'passive twink', and a *putito* ['little fag']. Comments such as these emphasise the perceived congruity between these models' youthful bodies, perceived to be unmasculine, and their mannerisms, self-presentation, and voice, all of which seem expected from their physical appearance in ways that Addison's effeminacy is not. Nearly all the viewers who comment on videos featuring Nicolas, Ariano, or Fox, and especially those from Spanish and Portuguese linguistic settings, are lenient towards the effeminacy these bottoms demonstrate.

It's almost certainly the case that the twink status of these Argentinian models helps drive this leniency towards their effeminacy. But even older effeminate bottoms are tolerated in some Latin American pornographic contexts in ways that would almost be unthinkable in Western contexts. The Argentinian studio, M2M Club, for example, features scenes in which a model called Ezebaires is paired with men whom we are told are bisexual *machos*. Invariably, Ezebaires is wholly sexually receptive and is described as a 'young bottom who lives to be fucked by dominant tops [and] loves to be used by machos to satisfy their lower instincts'.[2] Other terms used to describe Ezebaires include 'sissy effeminate pussyboy', 'very effeminate fag', 'bottom fag', and 'nice faggot'. Ezebaires is older, and not as twinky as the Argentinian models from Schoolboy Secrets and FamilyDick, although the studio at times still refers to him as a 'twink', which I suspect is a case of relexification, which in this case involves a new, Americanised label (*twink*) being substituted for an old Latin concept: *mariquita* or *pasivo* (Fernández-Alemany & Murray, 2002, p. viii; Galeano, 2022).

M2M Club offers viewers a hybrid pornographic experience in which global American pornographic language is used to represent traditional Latin American sexuality, in which masculine insertors fuck passive receptives. For example, in one video, 'Musti Fucks Ezebaires', the studio writes of 'another M2M-style explosive video. We coupled an ALPHA MALE, with capital letters, hairy, hung, and really dominant, with a passive fag who loves to be fucked by this type of males', with the lead image emphasising their opposite sex roles and gender expressions: the hirsute macho is stimulating his cock while Ezebaires is lying on his front, ass exposed, in a passive position (15 July 2019). Other images in this preview include gestures of dominance from the macho, such as the macho's hand placed firmly on Ezebaires's ass while Ezebaires sucks his cock. Importantly, in both images of Ezebaires being fucked – doggy and missionary – neither the macho nor Ezebaires is stimulating Ezebaires's penis. The whole focus is on the macho's cock and the 'fag's' ass (Fig. 3).

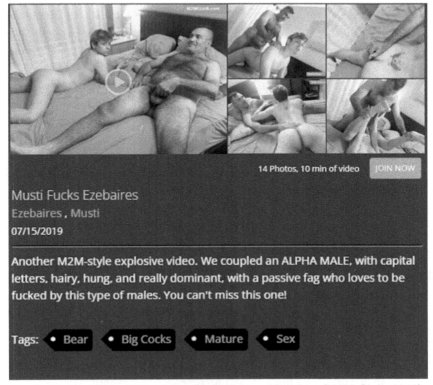

Fig. 3. Screenshot of 'Musti Fucks Ezebaires' Preview (M2M Club, 2019).

Ezebaires is thus made to represent 'all our bottom fags' who desire to be 'fucked by our bisexual macho[s]' (27 May 2019). Elsewhere, Ezebaires is paired with a model called BMF, which according to the studio represents an 'explosive couple: BMF, a typical dom Argentinian stud, lover of hard sex and sissy boys, and Ezebaires, a really nice sub bottom "twink", who gets all wet in the presence of an Alpha male like BMF' (1 May 2021).

These paratexts insist that only bottoms, and especially effeminate bottoms ('sissy boys'), are actually homosexual and effectively lack a functioning penis; instead they get 'all wet'. The 'typical' *machos* are said to be bisexual or 'heterocurious', which accords with the kind of *pasivo* fantasies documented by earlier anthropologists (Murray, 1995). In any case, by conjoining sex object choice, gender expression (as 'sissy' or 'effeminate'), and anal sex role preference as *passive*, M2M Club represents a radically different kind of porn studio to more mainstream North American ones such as Cocky Boys (Tannor Reed's studio), which largely organise their content based on sex object choice or anal sex role categories and eschew explicit links to gender presentation (though they may implicitly do so). Even though M2M Club uses words such as *twink* and *sub* in paratexts, these are often written in scare quotes, which suggests some unfamiliarity with the term. Interestingly, the studio adopts the use of a 'twink' tag for some of its videos, and sometimes this is applied to scenes inappropriately, where none of the models featured would be recognisable as a twink to North American audiences.

Ultimately, M2M Club, and to some extent Schoolboy Secrets, work by activating more traditional sexual fantasies indigenous to the Latin American contexts in which they operate, and which is vindicated by the sheer amount of Latin American viewers who comment on such videos when uploaded to sites such as XVideos. And when M2M uploads their own videos to XVideos, they use Anglicised words such as *queer*, *fairy*, and *faggot* as English translations of their own terms such as *mariquita*, to emphasise an older lineage of words that denote a conflation of gender, sex role and object choice.

While more traditional sexualities may present their own challenges to Western audiences in terms of distasteful or unwelcome gendered stereotypes, Western treatment of effeminate bottoms in gay porn also presents difficulties. By focusing overwhelmingly on sex object choice (gay porn vs. straight porn), and to a lesser extent on sex role (as top, bottom, or versatile), American and Western European gay porn is often inadequate when it comes to confronting the inevitable intrusion of unwanted gender expression into porn scenes. American models such as Bar Addison and Tannor Reed represent scapegoats for current insecurities around effeminacy, particularly among bottoms who either will not or cannot flip fuck and become sexually versatile, and therefore more obviously 'masculine' and thus belong and align with culturally dominant standards for gay masculinity. When it comes to written erotica, however, the situation is somewhat different, with fem bottoms beginning to take centre stage.

5.2 WRITING AND DESIRING FEM BOTTOMS

Written gay erotica on the internet is not nearly as prevalent or discoverable as visual gay porn, whether that be photos, cartoons or videos. But some websites archive written gay erotica in English, including, for the purposes of this book, the hypnosis fetish site Gay Spiral Stories and Menonthenet.com. Gay Spiral Stories frequently contains stories that focus on narratives of 'muscle theft', 'twinkification', or other kinds of feminisation, in which a masculine, muscular jock or otherwise 'straight-acting' man is stripped of his masculine identifiers and turns into an effeminate bottom, often with a twink body. These stories are certainly fetishistic because they focus specifically on the erotics of a specific practice: forms of feminisation or de-masculinisation, but for me they are also indicative of a broader interest in overturning American masc4masc paradigms and celebrating masculine and effeminate, heterogender pairings. The key element here is that the masc4masc dynamic becomes unsustainable under the weight of its own inauthenticity.

In the series 'Bimbo Boys', by Pup Don (2021), an average masculine man, Dan, transforms into an effeminate bottom, Danni. Described initially as a 'jeans and t-shirt kind of guy', he is presented physically and psychologically as a masculine gay man with little hint of any kind of effeminacy. However, after meeting a new neighbour, he mysteriously begins to change, physically and psychologically. He begins to want to shave and to look boyish and cute: 'He loved how cute he looked with a clean face and wondered why he let that icky stubble grow in all the time'. Now called Danni as opposed to Dan, his neighbour tells him:

> *'You've been taught your whole life what it means to be masculine, haven't you? From the time you learned what it meant to be gay you feared becoming the stereotype of the effeminate gay male. And as you made friends you reinforced all those ugly masculine traits in one another. Like a shield, a huge heavy coat that one would wear on a hot day. It's heavy and hot, it's a burden, isn't it. Think about how uncomfortable it is, Danni [...] Yes boy, all that masculinity is*

such a burden. It weighs heavy on your shoulders. You'd do anything to release it, wouldn't you, boy?'

Danni then meets Carlos, whom Danni's neighbour has also feminised in the same way as he is feminising Danni. Carlos was once a 'bearded rockabilly type' but after meeting Danni's neighbour, he becomes an effeminate twink bottom: 'Gone was his manly swagger replaced with a softer voice and more femme mannerisms. He now looked less like the kind of guy who ran an old school barber shop and more like one who worked in a stylish hair boutique in Boy's Town'. Carlos represents the male that Danni is slowly turning into as well. For both Carlos and Danni, their masculinity is seen as a burden, something inauthentic, whereas their effeminacy is seen as constituting who they really are.

Such a narrative questions the inevitability of gay men's attempts to masculinise and 'man up', and essentially reverses the cultural narratives penned by Matt Houlbrook (London) and George Chauncey (New York) in which queens and fairies become invisible by butching up due to the pressure to detach gender expression (as effeminate) from sex object choice (gay). Danni and Carlos return to the males they were born to be, personally and culturally.

In another story, 'SHORT: Seeds of a Twink Variety', by orrotica (2016), a masculine gay man, Tom, becomes an effeminate bottom twink, Tommy. Tom and his friend, Jack, are initially presented as jock-type *bros* who are both into fem twinks as sexual partners. While getting ready to go clubbing and go in search of twinks, Jack persuades Tom to give him a warm-up blowjob – something Tom wouldn't ordinarily do. While sucking off his friend, Tom begins to change. His body begins to de-masculinise: 'Sure enough his face was now clean-shaven…and the hair on his chest was nearly gone'. However, he still has his muscular physique. But then Tom goes back and deep-throats Jack, which seems to speed up the feminisation process. Now called Tommy, over the space of 20 minutes he 'lost focus on everything masculine that he once knew and began to focus on the dick and hairy body in front of him'. Jack now refers to Tommy as his 'faggy twink'.

This is a narrative that cannot contain two masculine gay men as partners, and therefore directly undermines the dominant American gay narrative that has been built up for decades, in which gay men must not imitate anything heterosexual and must both present as relatively masculine and/or as sexually versatile. In 'Seeds of a Twink Variety', a masc top and a fem bottom are presented as an erotic and sexually fulfilling partnership. Readers commenting on the story also found the dynamic erotic: 'Is it possible that the friends could

CONTINUE to drain his masculinity', wrote one, 'until he was a complete stereotype of the worst features of a SISSY: limp wristed, mincing, lisping'. This reader's comments effectively reverse the criticisms levelled against Bar Addison, whose limp-wristed, mincing personality is so reviled by viewers. In this story, however, Tommy's effeminacy is praised to the extent that the *worst* features of being a sissy are in fact desired as appropriate characteristics for Tommy: they belong *in* him.

In another story, 'From Bear to Fair (-y)' by Xanderboy (2008), the focus is on translating a macho, effeminophobic gay bear who surrounds himself with other machos into a gay club filled with effeminate twink bottoms, or fairies, as the title suggests. The bear in question, Robert, describes himself as a 'real man, not some skinny ass twink who can't handle any pipe smoke!' His friend, Karl, calls Robert out on his attitude to twinks and 'on the endless virtues of being macho'. Robert dismisses this criticism, referring to such twinks as 'little bitches who don't even know how to be a real man [...] I fucking hate those slutty twinks, never be caught dead sleeping with one...'. At this moment, a twinky queen enters the scene who embodies precisely the qualities that Robert has summarily dismissed. The twink grabs Robert's pipe and tosses it away: '"This won't do at all, honey," he commented, moving effeminately and his extremely tight clothes moving along with him as he sashayed'. Rather than transforming Robert into a fairy, though, the twink simply magically translates him into an uncomfortable setting in the hope that Robert's attitudes to fairies might change:

> 'Change of scenery, for realsies,' the queen was suddenly behind Robert, and this time had shiny, gossamer, and extremely gay wings sprouting out of his tight blue shirt with 'bitch' written on it. Suddenly Robert was in the middle of a big club, filled with skinny, half naked, perfect looking men frozen in the middle of dancing.

This short story is intended to be read from the perspective of the twinky queen or 'queeny boy', as the narrator refers to him at one point. From the queen's perspective, Robert is suffering under a pretence of masculinity. Robert is clearly gay (same-sex attracted) but has convinced himself that he will never fuck effeminate twinks because he imagines that gay is equivalent to an effeminate bottom.

As a 'solution', the 'twinky godmother' extracts Robert from his comfortable, macho space and moves him to a room full of fairies, in the hope that Robert may begin to change his mind about engaging with fairies and belong in company with them. I would suggest that the author specifically invokes traditional American names to describe effeminate bottoms, such as *fairy*, *bitch*, and *queen*, in order to offer the kind of defence of effeminate bottomhood that Robert desperately needs to accept.

Taken together, these stories on Gay Spiral Stories, among others, highlight the existence of, and desire for, narratives in which effeminate bottoms take centre stage in positive ways.[3] The dominant cultural insistence on mutual masculinity and sexual versatility is suspended, and pairings of masculine tops and fem bottoms are once again accepted as somehow natural.

The fetish of hypnosis, which is the dominant theme of Gay Spiral Stories, is therefore a literary device which is used to emphasise the extent to which gay men have already been 'programmed' to think that a macho form of masculinity is the gold standard to which all gay men have to conform themselves. These stories suggest, often via the entrance of a fem bottom into the narrative, that there are other ways to be gay, perhaps more authentic ways in which effeminacy and bottomhood belong together.

These stories are therefore an internal criticism of gay culture, rather than any meaningful statement on cultural attitudes outside the gay community. They question the certainty and truthfulness of masc gay identities, and seek to invoke more historical identities such as the *fairy* and *queen* as avenues for reclaiming a fem bottom identity in a gay culture that has routinely denigrated it for so long.

However, other forms of contemporary erotica create new ways to be a fem bottom without necessarily invoking older, historical labels and identities. In 'Pussyboy' by Greg Stone (2001), published on Menonthenet.com, a man called Greg celebrates the desirability of a 'pussyboy', Joey, who is depicted as an effeminate bottom.[4] Greg first encounters Joey in a restaurant, where Joey is waiting at tables. Through Greg's eyes, readers meet Joey as someone with 'a small build and rather effeminate mannerisms. The highly styled hair and close-fitting clothes suggested a flirtatious, even a vain character'. Greg refers to Joey as 'a real twink. A real little faggot', thereby determining Joey's sexuality based on external markers betraying his effeminacy, such as his clothes, his voice, and his mannerisms – all of which have traditionally been used by others to determine a man's sexuality (Loftin, 2007).

Greg introduces himself to Joey and slips a business card into his shirt pocket. Later, Joey heads round to Greg's apartment, where Greg seduces him. The erotic nature of the encounter emerges through the descriptions of the two males, which emphasise polarity between them. Greg is a conventionally masculine man, whereas Joey is marked out by his gender nonconformity and his status as sexually passive with men. When Greg fucks Joey, Joey begins to own his status as a fem bottom for masculine men:

> *At first a sharp pain radiated up from his ass to his head, and his wrists strained so hard at the handcuffs that they left red marks. But gradually the feeling was replaced with pure pleasure as the warm shaft continued to press deeper into him, invading his most private place and filling his effeminate young body with the masculine stiffness.*

In Chapter 2 of the story, the contrast between the softness of Joey's 'effeminate young body' and Greg's 'masculine stiffness' increases. Joey moves in to Greg's apartment and assumes a styled role as a 'wife', cooking for them both and being very domestic:

> *Joey daydreamed about the past couple of days as they drove around. He felt a little changed, as if he'd become something new, a different person determined by Greg's needs and passions. His anus had become a pussy, his mouth a tool for sucking cock, his hands, his nipples...all for Greg, for his cock and mouth.*[5]

Joey has become more than a gay bottom: he is a *pussyboy*, defined by his gender nonconformity and his anal sex role as a bottom. The two are mutually reinforced and Joey begins to feel deeply satisfied by being a *pussyboy* and enjoys being desired as such by Greg: 'Joey could not have been happier. Kneeling face-down on the bed one morning as his sugar daddy rimmed and doggy-fucked him, Joey thought about everything he had become, and all he had given up'.

What had he given up? The story seems to imply that Joey has given up all pretence at trying to be something he isn't and belongs comfortably with his effeminacy. While the story obviously creates a sexual fantasy narrative that readers are not expected to locate in real life in quite the same way as the fantasy envisages, the writer of this story nevertheless suggests that the story opens potentialities for gay sexual relationships in the US that are outside mainstream narratives. Greg is also positioned as a liminal figure, on the margins of gay culture, as a 'normal man' or 'real man' in the tradition of *trade*, discussed by Houlbrook (2005) and Chauncey (1994).

As I mentioned in Chapter 4 in relation to the rugby documentary, *Steelers*, Greg's journey to 'being gay' is likely to have been somewhat different to Joey's. Joey is likely to have experienced gender nonconformity since boyhood, be called a *fag* by other boys and identified more with girls and women, whereas Greg is likely to see his same-sex desire as the only thing making him different from other masculine typical men and may have had an otherwise unremarkable boyhood and adolescence. Joey's struggles – being bullied for being effeminate and probably gay from a young age – will have been different from Greg's – such as his likely struggle to really believe he is truly gay, because he's not effeminate, or dealing with other people's incredulity when he says he is actually gay. Nevertheless, in the space of this sexual fantasy, both pairs in the heterogender dyad find a way to belong with their sexuality. To global majority readers with a knowledge of more indigenous or traditional forms of homosexuality, Joey's and Greg's relationship would indeed be considered heterogender, and therefore in some kind of tension with contemporary masc4masc dynamics.

Non-Western tensions between traditional, heterogender and contemporary modes of male same-sex desire in written erotica have been identified by Arash Guitoo in his analysis of 'gay' stories on the Persian sexblog, shahvani.com (2021). Guitoo has analysed Persian sexual fantasy narratives to explore the lingering presence of indigenous and traditional ways of conceptualising male same-sex desire in Iran. Guitoo explores the identity of the *kūnī* in erotic stories, which can be translated as *faggot* (US) or *poof* (UK). The *kūnī* is a passive, effeminate male homosexual who has a fairly coherent identity in which sex object choice, anal sex role, and gender expression are mutually reinforcing. The *kūnī* is distinguished in these stories from the modern *gay* identity, and some users of the sexblog are keen to police the word *gay*, to avoid relexifying it to mean *kūnī*:

> *Why do you pollute the word gay? That what you are is called being 'faggot' (kūnī)! Gay is an emotional and sexual relationship between two men, in which the two have a reciprocal sexual relationship with each other. If one is only passive and the other is only active, it is called being 'faggot' (kūnī). If both are active and passive, it is called being gay. Please do not associate gay with such nonsense and bring it in disrepute. Please do not associate being gay with being 'faggot' (kūnī). (quoted p. 893)*

As Guitoo observes, this sexblog is currently a site of conflicting perspectives among Iranian male androphiles, some of whom wish to identify with the modern 'gay' identity, while others wish to retain an identity as *kūnī*, and thereby emphasise their self-awareness as an effeminate bottom. 'The modernist perspective', argues Guitoo, 'blames passive men in Iranian society who define their role according to a heterosexual relationship and like to see themselves as the feminine passive partner for reinforcing the structures of a repressive patriarchal system through their behaviour and self-perception' (pp. 895–896).

What's especially interesting here is that in this instance, the situation in male–male erotica is less accepting in non-Western settings. On Western sites such as Gay Spiral Stories, writers are writing against decades of erosion of a fem bottom identity, and as such attract readers who are largely enthusiastic with this project and seek out such stories specifically because they want this kind of content. Importantly, such readers are able to enthusiastically fantasise about masc–fem pairings from within a wider egalitarian societal context that wouldn't also seek to impose a host of negative social consequences in addition to being a fem bottom. By contrast, shahvani.com seems to be in the midst of a conflict where the destabilising of heterogender male homosexuality by self-identified gays is still very much in process, and therefore stories that continue to explore *kūnī* identities and desires receive strident support and vilification in equal measure.

It seems, then, that in the world of online porn and erotica, Western explorations of heterogender male homosexuality, which includes a fem bottom and a masc top, are at a moment of particular creativity and that stand at odds with Western LGBTQ+ media that continues to be suspicious of any equivalence between effeminacy and bottoming in males. The *pussyboy* identity in particular has been given extensive treatment on social media sharing sites such as Tumblr and more recently, Twitter/X and BDSMLr, and is emerging from its initial incubation in BDSM circles to wider gay community discussion and sexual fantasy. The next section explores sexual fantasy narratives on Tumblr that celebrate the *pussyboy* and its cognate identity, that of the *boiwife*.

5.3 PUSSYBOYS, BOIWIVES AND THEIR MEN

The pussyboy and boiwife nuance perspectives on effeminate bottoms in the West because they indicate interest in heterogender homosexuality, even if only in the realm of sexual fantasy, in a wider LGBTQ+ climate that is highly suspicious of such a dynamic.[6] The pussyboy and boiwife – as they are explored here – can be identified as bottoms but their form of bottomhood permeates their gender nonconforming identity in ways that will not apply to other bottoms.[7] The pussyboy and boiwife are thus identity consolidations which have arisen from a subsection of Western gay bottoms and they have primarily developed through online sexual fantasies which utilise both image and text, and which may or may not have direct correspondence to their offline sexual identities and practices (Barker, 2014; Norton, 2016).

Tumblr blogs circulating sexual fantasies associated with pussyboys and boiwives do so, for better or worse, as part of a broader gay BDSM culture that has now largely migrated from Tumblr to other platforms such as BDSMlr and Twitter/X, due to Tumblr's crackdown of adult content in December 2018. Most of these blogs are run by users who self-identify as a pussyboy or boiwife, and their posts and/or blog bios use these terms frequently. A few blogs in this genre are also run by users who self-identify as masculine lovers of pussyboys and boiwives and their output offers a broader picture of who the pussyboys and boiwives are in dialogue with, and how their fantasies intersect with those of the men or 'Daddies'.

Pussyboys and boiwives on Tumblr present as recognisably male rather than typically female, and most identify as gay. One blogger encapsulates this fem bottom identity when they say: 'As a boy who wants to be a wife to a dominant Man, I want to embody all the traditional roles – my Husband won't ever have to worry about not coming home to a clean house, an uncooked dinner, or a smooth pussy'. This blogger specifically identifies as a boiwife and has thought hard about their identity as a fem bottom: 'Males can be girls too', they argue, 'and that's perfectly ok. And some males only want to be girls to their respective Man, but still be a male to everyone else. And that's ok too'. Equally, this blogger is adamant that while they value those 'girls' who have made 'that final plunge and truly switch[ed]' to presenting as a woman, this blogger nevertheless still identifies as a gay male.

Another blogger arrives at a similar perspective concerning their overall identity – effeminate and gay, but still male rather than female. In their blog bio, this blogger expresses a desire for an 'Alpha Male willing to wife me up', and in one of their posts, they explain that part of the joy of being with a 'real man' is that 'I can let myself be effeminate around him and others. I can be the girl he needs as much as he's the man I need'. This blogger identifies as '100% bottom and submissive', and, as with some of the global majority effeminate bottoms explored in this book, is attracted to hyper-masculine men: 'I love hairy beefy dominant men'. Indeed, they express an idea shared by non-Western fem bottoms, which insists that being anally penetrated is integral to being 'wifed up': the act of being anally penetrated in part constitutes this new status as being different to masculine men.

In terms of sex object choice, boiwives and pussyboys typically express a uniform desire for males completely unlike them along certain correlates, such as muscularity and hirsuteness, emphasised by frequently capitalising 'Men', to distinguish between themselves, who are only phenotypically men, and Men, who are also socially and culturally recognised as 'real men'. One blogger believes that 'sissyboys like me are naturally attracted to Strong Men'.

In another post, this blogger explains that 'pussyboys love all things masculine. A Man's hairy chest, his muscles, and of course his cock'; they 'love being picked up by Alpha Males like this. Knowing their Man's arms are strong enough to easily pick them up and Manhandle them like a sissy is such a turn on'. Another blogger suggests in a similar vein that 'Men have big pecs to serve as pillows for their boywives'.

These bloggers' sex object choice is complemented by their fantasies of sexual submissiveness and anal receptivity. They embody what another blogger said more generally of bottoms:

> ...bottom is both a 'gender' and a 'sexual orientation.' It's a comprehensive identity and way of life, based on embracing one's natural femininity and receptivity, one's inferiority to and complementarity to Men. A true bottom turns her receptivity according to Nature into freely chosen and actualised complete acceptance.

As with the historical *fairy* or the contemporary *kothi*, for these Western pussyboys and boiwives, their desire to be sexually penetrated by a 'real man' also explains their gender presentation. Their desire for powerful, strong and typically masculine men leads these bloggers to present in ways that they believe will entice men to penetrate them. As Kulick noted about the Brazilian *travestis* he studied, 'it is thus in the bed where gender is truly established' (Kulick, 1998, p. 126).

One blogger in particular has published several sex scenarios in which fem bottoms such as boiwives and pussyboys are ravished by dominant, masculine men because they perceive their boiwives' sexual penetrability. In one of these, a male character called Misha sits waiting patiently on a bed for her new husband, Aleksandr, who is 'tall, dark, muscular'. As Aleksandr enters the marriage bedroom,

> ...the sight of his young virgin bride all naked and ready to be taken sent fire to his loin. What beauty. What innocence. What softness. Aleksandr couldn't wait to mount him and sink his manhood into his boiwife's virgin cunt, impregnating her on her marriage day.

This narrative invokes a stereotypical Russian or pan-Slavic context which, for Western audiences, perhaps contrasts with the more egalitarian context from which the blogger writes. In this Slavic world where traditional gender roles remain (or at least they do so in this fantasy), the only option for a submissive fem bottom like Misha is for her not only to be anally penetrated by a masculine, muscular man, but to be 'impregnated', by which is inferred the depositing of semen in her body after being fucked anally, typically referred to in this genre as being 'bred'.

The mention of marriage is also significant because especially for boiwives, part of their identity is centred on at least the aspiration to a long-term monogamous union with a masculine man, and this in turn contributes to the number of domestic fantasies through which the boiwives express their gender and which also takes the focus away from only being fucked. The emphasis on domesticity radically re-writes decades of Western gay activism which has been explicitly suspicious of heteronormative domestic settings and the institution of marriage. The contemporary boiwife and pussyboy push back against such gay activism because they feel that, at least for them, and if only in their fantasies, a heterogender form of homosexuality is entirely apt and indeed liberating.

Together, these sexual fantasies circulated by boiwives and pussyboys on Tumblr, who may also at times simply identify as bottoms or with other related but distinct terms such as *sissyboy* or *femboy*, help create a narrative which enables these bloggers combine to emphasise the interconnections between their sex object choice, their sex role, and their gender nonconforming presentations in ways that others can readily identify with. These are not simply gay males who enjoy bottoming: they are self-identified fem bottoms who exclusively seek to be penetrated by dominant, masculine men and in such a union, to adopt a stereotypical – even exaggerated – role traditionally associated in Europe and North America with women.

In some ways, by invoking stereotyped images of post-industrial liberal domesticity, these bloggers are quite conservative in their ambitions. But on the other hand, they are also subversive. These fem bottoms are writing against a deluge of other gay voices around them telling them that their fantasies are warped, wrong, outdated, patriarchal, heteronormative, limited or simply disturbing (Vytniorgu, 2024a).

One of the persistent criticisms of heterogender homosexuality posited by ethnographers in the past has been that as an ideal type, it's the product of an effeminate bottom's fantasy: *locas*, *maricas* and even *queens* and *fairies* love the idea that the man penetrating them is 'normal' – a conventional man – and it's only they who are different and 'not-men' (Cardoso, 2005; Fernández-Alemany & Murray, 2002; Murray, 2000). Any sign that the man might want his ass to be touched or might want to touch the bottom's genitals, then they are rejected: the illusion is broken.

All this would suggest that the men who fuck such bottoms have no real voice, and until the Honduran study by Fernández-Alemany and Murray (2002), ethnographers in Latin America found it extremely difficult to interview *machos* or *hombres* because of their apparent invisibility. However, *pussyboys* and *boiwives* on Tumblr, and now on Twitter/X and elsewhere, interact with the men, or Daddies, they find attractive, and these men – who may or may not identify as gay – circulate their own fantasies of being with a fem bottom, thereby complicating the assertion that these ideal types are only being pushed from one direction.

The Daddies and men play a key role in their blogging in affirming the fem identities of the boiwives and pussyboys who ardently follow them and reblog their posts. One blogger explains how 'I love you for exactly the wifely qualities that made you feel rejected by others'. In a similar vein, another Daddy writes how he can't get enough effeminacy in a desired male partner: 'As a real butch bear masc daddy, I love flaming femme fags, they're what I'm naturally attracted to. The queenier a faggot is; the more likely I will be into him'. This text acts as a caption to a GIF of the Canadian singer Shawn Mendes, who is depicted seated and 'talking with his hands' in what can be perceived to be a stereotypically effeminate way (Daniele et al., 2020; Ravenhill & de Visser, 2017). For this Daddy, Mendes's perceived effeminacy is extremely attractive, and he desires all latently effeminate bottoms to become more feminised.

Blogging about their fantasies using an online microblogging platform such as Tumblr or Twitter/X also enables the Daddies and men who desire fem bottoms to feel affirmed in their own identity and masculinity. They cannot take their desirability, power or dominance for granted. Rather, by dialoguing with fem bottoms through reblogs and comments on posts, both halves of the heterogender union can be strengthened in the validity of their sexual desires. As one Daddy explains, a boiwife's 'pussy is much more to me than a simple pleasure source. It's my home and comfort in a trying world, my safe place, nurturing me in body and soul, to help me be the man you deserve'. For another, 'a good man's reward is a submissive pussyboy desperate to serve him and treat him like a king the moment he walks in the door'.

What is beyond question is that the Daddies here clearly have sexual desire for types of gay males that in more mainstream Western gay culture are frequently touted as undesirable sexual partners. For these men, they really do want fem, fem, fem in their bottoms. As one blogger puts it: 'sissy femme bois are my hearts [*sic*] deepest, longest inferring desire'. That boiwives and pussyboys desire them in return is equally affirming. Indeed, these fem bottoms explicitly desire presentations of traditional masculinity or manliness that in other Western contexts may be looked upon with suspicion as outdated, patriarchal and antithetical to a modern feminist vision for gender equality. In some ways, these contemporary fem bottoms have managed to break free of the endogamous trap of only having a pool of other self-identified gays from which to date, who may be 'too fem' and/or sexually versatile to be attractive to these fem bottoms. These fem bottoms allow their penetrative men to 'engage in homosexual practices [fucking and being sucked] on their own terms' and seek to validate, not undermine or question, their man's desire to be seen as manly or masculine (Hekma et al., 1995, p. 28).

5.4 FEM BOTTOMS BELONGING TOGETHER

What's especially interesting is the way in which pussyboy and boiwife sexual fantasies seem to be categorised as kink or as part of the wider gay BDSM culture, whereas in fact they seem to fit squarely within more mainstream homosexual dynamics once one looks beyond Western cultural contexts. Indeed, as Stephen Murray points out, on the broader world stage, it's the Western, egalitarian (masc4masc, sexually versatile) form of homosexuality that's the cultural anomaly – the 'kink', if you like (2000; 1995). As far as I can tell, the pussyboy and boiwife aren't hugely different in self-described characteristics and desires from those of heterogender Latin *pasivos* described elsewhere in this book, or from those of the Indian and Bangladeshi *kothis*. Historically, they resemble the *fairy*, *queen* and *pansy* of Anglo-American history. If heterogender homosexual dynamics are considered kinky, relegated to murky corners of the internet, then this arguably reveals more about the culture that designates such dynamics as kinky than the so-called kinky desires themselves.

On Tumblr and Twitter/X, pussyboy and boiwife sexual fantasies circulate in a similar way to the heterogender written erotica discussed in the previous section. This content is deliberately sought out by English-speaking users predominantly based in North America and Europe who cannot easily see themselves or their desires in more mainstream gay porn and the wider culture offline, so must turn to online platforms that circulate the material they want, but which is also often situated among material that is distinctly different in tone and content. As a result, heterogender gay fantasies must now compete for attention among quite different fantasies that are more easily identifiable as kink, including dominance/submission, chastity and fetish fantasies that use the language of *faggot*, *slave* and *master* and often feature two recognisably masculine gay males rather than the masculine top/effeminate bottom dynamic focused on in this book (Wignall, 2022). Frequently, fem bottoms and the men who desire them insist that their heterogender preferences are not a kink or fetish, and resent that their sexual preferences are offered alongside more 'extreme' content that some may argue degrades and objectifies fem bottoms.

It seems, though, that the identities of *pussyboy* and *boiwife* are likely to remain, for the time being, in the arena of gay sexual fantasy rather than enter more mainstream gay slang. However, I would insist that such identities belong as creative latter day reinventions of more established but perhaps less visible Anglophone identities such as *queen*, *swish*, *fairy* or *nelly*, that also embody a variety of non-sexual connotations and dynamics as well as sexual ones. The central dynamics of the newer identities are demonstrably similar to those of the older but more well-known identities. Such dynamics include an insistence on the interconnecting nature of sex object choice, gender expression and sex role as a personal, social and cultural positioning in the world. Effeminacy and sexual receptivity are felt to be mutually reinforcing. These are males who see themselves as male, or even in some contexts as men, but who also feel in some profound way that they are not like other men in their culture, and identify quite strongly with more female-typical or female-stereotyped roles, aesthetics and identities while simultaneously creating a distinctly 'faggy' subjectivity that materialises in concrete tropes, behaviours and language(s).

Most pussyboys and boiwives do not cross-dress, or only do so with underwear, and few wear make-up: their identification with femininity seems more deep-seated and is intimately connected to how they see themselves or wish to see themselves in relation to the masculine men they seek as sexual and romantic partners. In this instance, gender nonconformity is deliberately explored alongside same-sex sexual and romantic desires. That is: they are same sex, but heterogender. As I discussed in Chapter 1 in relation to the difference between *effeminate* and *feminine*, pussyboys and boiwives are usually unmistakably *male*; they are considered effeminate because their femininity is refracted through maleness, which is partly why the Daddies and men who desire them are so interested in them. The pussyboys and boiwives are males, but they're emphatically not *men* like the Daddies are.

As such, pussyboys and boiwives represent an emerging attempt among gay-identified males in the West to search for opportunities to express their desires and identities in ways that may in fact be made easier if they could also access historical and cross-cultural examples of heterogender same-sex unions and identities, as explored in this book (see the case of Samantha Hudson in Chapter 4). As the novelist Neil Bartlett has written, 'all the time, I think, we want to find out about each other, to know if we really belong to each other, belong together' (1988, p. xx). Erotic models such as Bar Addison or Tannor Reed make sense when set within a broader context: they are not some 'effeminate broken third wheel', as one porn viewer commented about Reed. They 'belong together', along with models such as Nicolas, Ariano, Fox or Ezebaires, the pussyboys and boiwives online, and the writers of erotic heterogender gay sexual fantasies on Gay Spiral Stories. Online sexual fantasies provide a way for fem bottoms to explore modes of belonging together, of invoking a sense of shared desires, identities, bodies and group identity. They allow fem bottoms and those who desire them to re-connect sexuality and gender in ways that feel authentic for them and may, crucially, take them both outside of the online world into a more fully embodied and authentic offline world of sexual encounters and relationships.

And modelling also emerges here as a key creative practice in which to re-assert the coherence of a male body and effeminate presentation, which is so often stigmatised as *not* belonging in a male body. Indeed, both modelling and viewing, and then commenting on uploaded videos, represent routes to new knowledge that may lead to belonging offline as well as online. This is not empirical knowledge, but a form of *carnal resonance*: tactile, visceral attachment and aroused attention to a way of being, feeling and seeing, that leads to new languages, identities and even belonging (Paasonen, 2011).

The final chapter explores how effeminate belonging in the different places and spaces explored in this book relates to the emerging theme of sexual wellbeing as distinct from sexual health. Bottoms, and fem bottoms in particular, may confront emotions of shame due to embodying and practising stigmatised behaviours and identities. How might some of the places and spaces discussed in this book impact fem bottoms' sexual wellbeing and what might professionals and practitioners in health, educational and third-sector environments do to adapt them to enhance sexual wellbeing?

NOTES

1. Translations are the author's own.
2. https://www.m2mclub.com/models/Ezebaires.html (accessed 26 July 2022).
3. See also: https://www.gayspiralstories.com/story/show/430057; https://www.gayspiralstories.com/story/show/455945; as well as stories by Ethan White on https://ethanwhite.indieerotica.com/, especially 'Nothing too Extreme' (https://ethanwhite.indieerotica.com/2019/01/20/nothing-too-extreme/) and 'What a Boi Wants' (https://ethanwhite.indieerotica.com/2018/10/21/what-a-boi-wants/) (accessed 16 August 2022).
4. http://eroticstories.menonthenet.com/index.cfm?m=article&ArticleRecId=294439 (accessed 16 August 2022).
5. http://eroticstories.menonthenet.com/index.cfm?m=article&ArticleRecId=294440 (accessed 16 August 2022).
6. For an extended version of this section, please see Vytniorgu (2023a).
7. I am aware that the term *pussyboy* is also used in different contexts by some trans men to articulate a gay identity.

6

EFFEMINATE BELONGING AND SEXUAL WELLBEING

This chapter explores the importance of belonging for sexual wellbeing among bottoms who are gender nonconforming in various ways. It begins by highlighting the shift of attention from sexual health to the more expansive paradigm of sexual wellbeing, before indicating how effeminate belonging might contribute to sexual wellbeing in some of the places and spaces and contexts explored earlier in the book. The chapter is intended to be of particular relevance to professionals and practitioners working in health, educational and LGBTQ+ settings.

6.1 FROM SEXUAL HEALTH TO SEXUAL WELLBEING

In the 1990s and 2000s, the literature on gay men's health was, perhaps understandably, overwhelmingly related to HIV prevention and public health strategies, especially in non-Western contexts in which sexual health literacy was considered poor, but where the very concept of *gay* or *LGB* was also haphazardly known, except for middle-class men who were able to travel to Western gay communities (Boyce, 2007; Murray, 1995; Parker, 1999). In the 2010s, scholarly interest in gay men's sexual health in global majority settings retained a focus on sexually transmitted infection (STI) prevention and the uptake of drugs such as pre-exposure prophylaxis (PrEP) that can prevent the transmission of HIV, but is now also interested in how variables such as sexual positioning (top, bottom or versatile sexual practice) shape gay, bisexual and men who have sex with men (MSM) risk and health-seeking behaviour (Ayala et al., 2013; Rios et al., 2019).

Unsurprisingly, bottoms have been identified, both historically and today, as being especially at risk of contracting not just HIV but other STIs as well (DeVore, 2022). More specifically, *twinks* (young-looking, slender gay men), who are reported to bottom and self-identify as bottoms more than other gay subtypes, are even more at risk (Lyons & Hosking, 2014). This has meant that bottoms, and especially twink bottoms, who are routinely thought to be effeminate, are singled out as being somehow aligned with health-impeding and risky behaviours (Vytniorgu, 2024b).

While it's understandable that health practitioners want to do their best to help at-risk populations and improve public health literacy about modes of STI transmission and risky sexual practices, it's also the case that a focus on sexual health and sexual health education may inadvertently impede broader sexual wellbeing, including experiences of belonging for gender nonconforming gay bottoms. Incessant communications around risk and disease can exacerbate experiences of shame anxiety and the anticipation of stigma (Dolezal, 2021). As Angela Jones has argued more broadly, sexual science researchers have often overlooked the importance of pleasure and how such erasure is also connected to the erasure of marginalised 'racial, gendered, classed, and sexual identities' (2019, p. 643). In practice, this can mean that consideration of nuanced sexual and gendered identities is virtually shut down.

Moreover, the overwhelming *gay* and *LGBTQ+*-centric nature of public health prevention for men who have sex with men in non-Western settings means that there is also a risk of misunderstanding or under-appreciating indigenous sexual identities and practices that contribute to sexual wellbeing, which may focus especially on the interrelationship between sex role as a bottom and gender expression as fem or effeminate (Stief, 2017).

Lewis et al. have suggested that key components of sexual wellbeing include 'comfort with sexuality', 'sexual self-esteem' and 'sexual self-respect', all of which highlight the way in which people's sexual wellbeing is mediated by engagement with others and the wider culture (2021, p. 609). Sexual wellbeing, these authors argue, should be seen as 'a distinct and revolutionary concept that challenges our accepted thinking', moving well beyond the idea of sexual wellbeing as merely a component of sexual health (p. 608).

Attention to sexual wellbeing among fem bottoms, therefore, would need to consider the impact of shame and stigma on bottoms in a range of spaces, and how the wider culture may be affecting bottoms' comfort with sexuality and gender expression, not just in primary care and sexual health settings where bottoms can face challenges associated with shame anxiety (Kutner et al., 2021; Winder, 2023). For gender nonconforming bottoms, the anticipation of shame or experienced stigma can involve fears that their sexual identity and desires will not be validated or that their gender expression, in combination with their sex role preferences, will be repudiated even by those such as other gay men with whom they might otherwise seek to belong.

It therefore seems important that LGBTQ+ health and wellbeing practitioners in both educational and health spaces anticipate some of the ways in which sexual wellbeing experiences impact other aspects of the self and may cause emotional or relational difficulty in seemingly unrelated areas of life (Dolezal, 2022). And, as Ron Schleifer and Jerry Vannatta have argued in relation to health care, but which also applies elsewhere, narratives and stories are particularly important for attuning to the complexities of someone's identity; disciplinary traditions from literary and cultural studies emphasise the importance of ambiguity, attentive listening and responsive engagement – all of which are critical for professionals who meet with gay boys and men to talk about their experiences (2019).

6.2 BODIES, EXPECTATIONS AND ENVIRONMENTAL CONTEXT

Some of the narratives explored in Chapter 4 highlighted the ways in which homophobia and sex-object choice dominate media perceptions of sexual prejudice among gay men while also colouring the nature of autobiographical reflections of past abuse by gender nonconforming gay men. Whereas a book such as Paul Harfleet's *Pansy Boy* or the French film, *Reinventing Marvin*, is explicit about the way in which a boy's effeminacy or gender nonconformity might provoke bullying in a school and/or domestic space, the documentary *Olly Alexander: Growing Up Gay*, or the film *Everybody's Talking About Jamie*, subordinates gender expression and potential sex role preferences to a focus on sex object choice (being gay). To be sure, these texts offer emotive and sensitive depictions of young gay men's experiences of hostile spaces of non-belonging in school that in any case can be instructive for professionals. But by failing to tackle the real reason why the protagonists experience non-belonging – because of their effeminacy, rather than their homosexuality, per se – these texts fail to establish an important link between effeminate belonging and sexual wellbeing that may be especially helpful for improving engagement with gender nonconforming gay boys and men.

For gender nonconforming gay youth especially, it's often the case that it's their gender nonconformity and 'question marks' around possible sexual receptivity that provoke hostile reactions among peers. For that reason, schools and other educational spaces need to be responsive to the varied reasons why young gay males may be targeted by bullies and what impact this bullying may have on such boys' developing sense of sexual wellbeing, such as sexual self-esteem and self-respect. Effeminophobia, or femmephobia, will be just as relevant as homophobia, and it will be the intersectional experience of both that creates the unique threats to sexual wellbeing among gender non-conforming gay youth who are beginning to explore their sexual fantasies and identities.

As Chapters 2, 4 and 5 also demonstrate, LGBTQ+ communities, both online and offline, can also be spaces of non-belonging and marginalisation for fem bottoms, who negotiate cultural and historical legacies and anxieties around gender expression and sex role that regularly find new incarnations in a range of contexts. Openly gay celebrities such as Olly Alexander and Troye Sivan have spoken publicly about their anxieties around labels such as *bottom* and *twink* – anxieties which largely circulate within LGBTQ+ communities rather than outside them and which cannot be understood properly without understanding the historical context in which these terms developed. As I argued in Chapters 4, 5 and elsewhere (Vytniorgu, 2024b), fem bottoms, many of whom are characterised rightly or wrongly in the media as *twinks*, face antipathy in gay communities for perpetuating what other gay men see as an anachronistic, outdated heteronormative stereotype about effeminate gay men being bottoms. Such criticism is elevated when these bottoms express a desire for a heterogender relationship with a masculine, 'straight-acting' man.

While I recognise that for many, perhaps even most, middle-class gay men in Anglo-American settings, the 'fem bottom' image of a *nelly queen* is distinctly distasteful, the often aggressive denigration of any possible synergy between fem gender expression and bottom sex role preference and identity can severely impede the development of sexual wellbeing and belonging among fem bottoms. As I explore in Chapter 5, the porn model, Bar Addison, for example, has often been criticised by viewers for being too effeminate and therefore perpetuating stereotypes about bottoms being 'mincing nelly machines'. He is not alone. Other white, American models such as Tannor Reed, Ryan Evans or Leo Grand have also faced negative comments that create a hostile space for others looking to identify through sexual fantasy with fem bottoms – to find others who may be like you. If LGBTQ+ media and the wider culture continue to demonise or denigrate fem bottoms, particularly those that desire heterogender unions with masculine tops, the basic message will be: you can't identify this way – it's wrong; and anyway, why on earth would you *want* to identify with such an outdated image of being gay?

The situation in global majority non-Western places and spaces is somewhat different, however, and is one of the major reasons why I have included discussion of these alongside Western narratives. The *kothis* described in Chapter 4, for example, have conflicted opinions about Western gay identities and narratives, which were often circulated by public health experts keen to raise awareness of HIV prevention strategies. What seems clear is that the largely Western rejection of effeminate bottom identity and heterogender homosexuality is not easily assimilated in non-Western settings. As Stephen Murray wrote in 2000, 'no one in societies in which gender-variant roles arise shares the Western analytical concern with specifying whether gender or sexuality is more important in defining these kinds of people' (p. 293). In Latin America, for example, where the Mediterranean narrative of heterogender homosexuality has profoundly shaped homosexual behaviour and identity for decades, there are still cultural scripts which allow for synergies between gender nonconformity and bottom sexual practice and identity.

Paratexts written on porn sharing websites in Spanish and Portuguese about the erotic models Ariano and Ezebaires, for example, are largely comfortable with the ways in which these models present themselves. The Argentinian porn studio, M2M Club, actively invokes heterogender homosexual narratives by positioning Ezebaires as an effeminate *fag* and his insertive partners as bisexual or heterosexual *machos*. Within the realm of sexual fantasy, these gendered and sexual identities and languages allow for effeminate belonging in ways that seem almost impossible in more Western-informed settings. In terms of sexual wellbeing, sexual respect is paradoxically accorded fem bottom models in these contexts, even when using otherwise abusive language such as *fag* or *marica*.

This raises important questions for professionals in Anglo-American settings around cultural norms and expectations. While Anglo-American gay men may strongly reject what they perceive to be homophobic language and imagery – at least in non-fantasy contexts – others may actively welcome it as part of their sexual wellbeing and sense of belonging. Even the Spanish actor, Samantha Hudson, who is also able to draw on a complex interplay of Mediterranean language and imagery when talking about himself, proudly stresses how the synergy of effeminate gender expression and bottom sexual practices coalesce in his sense of sexual wellbeing. Both are important to his life story and current self-image. In Anglo-American settings, scholars have noted the ways in which otherwise abusive language, such as *faggot* and *sissy*, have been repurposed in online kink and fantasy contexts, which provide gay men with a complex platform to explore content that, in this context, is distinctly erotic (Florêncio, 2020; Wignall, 2022).

Moreover, it's important to highlight the ways in which belonging and marginalisation are contextual, change over time and can sometimes occur simultaneously depending on context, thereby impacting sexual wellbeing in distinctive ways. In other words, sense of belonging and its impact on sexual wellbeing is not an unchanging state: it is shaped over time by engagement with environmental factors in shifting places and spaces. For example, in *Reinventing Marvin*, the young Marvin experiences effeminophobic abuse from his school peers and his family: they sense that he is a *tapette* and punish him accordingly for failing to aspire to and enact culturally dominant standards of masculinity. However, as Marvin grows into an adult, his early experiences of non-belonging and marginalisation help inform his adult sexual behaviour. As a boy and as an adult, Marvin employs autobiographical framing devices to story his emerging sexual and gendered identity, often subtly re-writing aspects in his search for sexual wellbeing and sexual self-respect and recognition from others. Eventually, he achieves a precarious balance between belonging and non-belonging, realising that both of these have been important in shaping his quest for sexual wellbeing.

In the written erotica explored in Chapter 5, narrative structures in which a formerly masculine man is transformed into an effeminate bottom enact a transformation from one sense of sexual wellbeing to another, in which effeminate belonging takes centre stage. Sexual fantasy narratives such as 'Bimbo Boys' and 'SHORT: Seeds of a Twink Variety' both use a transformation device to show how previous notions of sexual wellbeing (sexual self-esteem) as a masculine man were, in this instance, somewhat deceptive and concealed a more authentic sense of self. For both Carlos and Danni in 'Bimbo Boys', their masculinity is seen as a burden, something inauthentic, whereas their effeminacy is seen as constituting who they really are. Such a narrative questions the inevitability of gay men's attempts to masculinise and 'man up'. Danni and Carlos return to the males they were born to be, personally and culturally, and in the process establish the importance of belonging with effeminacy and bottoming as key to a new sense of sexual wellbeing.

Other narratives employ relatively new terms such as *boiwife* and *pussyboy* to imagine and fantasise about new ways to belong with effeminacy and bottom subjectivity and practice, and in the process enhance the sexual wellbeing of self-identified *boiwives* and *pussyboys* and the men who desire them. Online communities on microblogging platforms such as Twitter/X and Tumblr can represent counterpublics that critique what users consider to be the dominant 'masc4masc' paradigm in which two sexually versatile, masculine presenting men form the gold standard gay couple image. Speaking into and against such a dominant narrative, pussyboys and boiwives and the men who desire them use sexual fantasies combining text and image to affirm gender complementary or heterogender unions between 'masc top' and 'fem bottom'. As one blogger has written:

> ...*bottom is both a 'gender' and a 'sexual orientation.' It's a comprehensive identity and way of life, based on embracing one's natural femininity and receptivity, one's inferiority to and complementarity to Men. A true bottom turns her receptivity according to Nature into freely chosen and actualised complete acceptance.*

Such statements are intended to be encouraging to the boiwives and pussyboys who follow this blog and who are invited to imagine visual and textual representations and possibilities to enhance their sexual self-esteem and belong with their bodies as male, but not necessarily as 'men'. In a wider culture that routinely questions the possibility and desirability of conjoining gender expression and sex role preference into an identity to belong with, these online sexual fantasy communities represent important ways in which users negotiate new possibilities for effeminate belonging.

Where LGBTQ+ counsellors have advocated the need to understand the importance of gay men's 'tribes' and subgroups (Maki, 2017; Neves & Davies, 2023) in the context of a sex-positive professional encounter, there is also a need to consider the ways in which the search for effeminate belonging and sexual wellbeing may impact men's broader outlook on sexuality and LGBTQ+ issues. As I explored in Chapter 1, LGBTQ+ media routinely attempts to engineer a shift in attitudes towards bottoms and bottoming. On the one hand, commentators seek to tackle the shame and stigma around bottoming and being a bottom, which is to be welcomed for any male who engages in receptive anal sex. However, adjacent attempts to detach bottoming from any gender expression, or to emphasise the superiority of masculine 'power bottoms' who flout stereotypes of effeminate bottoms, mean that the quest for effeminate belonging as a bottom is cultural as well as personal. Twitter/X, Tumblr and other social networking websites such as Reddit and the gay porn kink website, BDSMLr, afford fem bottoms and the men who desire them to form a constellation of counterpublics that re-imagine gender and sexual relations outside of what is felt to be a constricting consensus about sexual versatility and the rejection of the very stereotypes that in fact constitute the fantasies of some fem bottoms (Vytniorgu, 2024a).

It's not uncommon, therefore, to find content that imagines relationships of asymmetry between a 'real man' and a *boiwife*, which re-works cultural legacies of domesticity that elsewhere in LGBTQ+ media are routinely and forcefully rejected as being dangerously heteronormative and even anti-feminist. As such, it seems crucial that any mental health, educational or sexual wellbeing practitioner who engages with men and boys who align themselves with these identities, experiences and fantasies seeks to understand the overall logic and context within which these identities and fantasies are consolidated. Young people experiencing confusion or distress around their sexual and gendered identities may do so precisely because, in their context, they do not have access to cultural sanctions for the kinds of desires and fantasies they feel drawn to.

Indeed, it may also be expedient to keep an open mind as to the possible ways in which fem bottom identity, experience and desire may intersect with other subversive stances on cultural or political issues, especially around race and the body. There is a strain of valuable research in gender and sexuality studies that has understandably critiqued the ways in which certain ethnicities and racialised bodies are sexualised, often in ways felt to be disempowering – especially for Asian gay men (Nguyen, 2014). However, it may also be the case that for others, it's precisely the intersection of various 'minority' characteristics that energises sexual fantasy and consolidates sexual and gendered role identities.

For example, there are a cluster of blogs on Twitter/X, Tumblr and BDSMLr that create and circulate fantasies of Arab or Muslim supremacy, where physically imposing, muscular, hirsute men voice 'traditional' views about marriage and seek or are sought by white fem bottom males who identify as a *pussyboy* or *boiwife*. One blogger on Twitter/X, who identifies as a Muslim Daddy, writes alongside a GIF of a white twink, who is referred to using she/her pronouns, fellating another man: 'The liberal would look at her and see oppression. In reality, she is as happy and content as ever'. On Tumblr, the same blogger notes how 'real men', especially Arab men from the Middle East, don't 'take shit from gay bottoms, especially flamboyant ones'. While the tone of much of this blogger's content is firm about the roles of 'Western faggots', this blogger's primary aim is to dispel myths about Muslim men, to question de-centre Western liberal attitudes about gay liberation and to imagine scenarios in which Anglo-American or Western European gay bottoms become devoted boiwives to a non-Western Muslim man.

In one story that acts as a caption to an image of a naked couple (Arab man and white boiwife), the blogger notes how:

> She [the boiwife] was reluctant at first. The only thing she had heard of Muslim men were those horrible things that came from the TV. When she met Omar everything changed. He was a refugee on public money who attended some of the same classes as her in university. She learned how cultured and sophisticated his once

> *seemingly backward customs were. She adapted to them slowly and without even noticing. She stopped pursuing an education, moved in with him, and became every day more obedient, assuming responsibility for the feminine roles in his home.*

In some ways, this narrative resembles the transformation stories on Gay Spiral Stories, where a gay man's mindset changes due to input from someone new in his life. Here, the blogger rewrites dominant narratives of Muslim assimilation to Western ideals of liberalism by positioning the Muslim in a position of authority over the Western gay bottom (Lambevski, 1999). The setting is also significant: an American university, presumably a bastion of traditional liberal values, is the space in which this unexpected transformation and learning begins.

Such narratives are undoubtedly challenging for many Anglo-American readers. However, it seems important to suspend judgement before the overall context and purpose is established. As the LGBTQ+ media articles discussed in Chapter 1 highlight, it's tempting for contemporary audiences to impose or universalise a set of attitudes that will help progress liberation for those deemed oppressed, such as the maligned, stereotyped effeminate bottom. But there may be some contexts in which asserting these attitudes may not be especially helpful and may not contribute to sexual wellbeing or feelings of effeminate belonging for the men in question. Attention to how intersections of gender, sex role preferences, class, ethnicity and much more shape fem bottom identities need not necessitate a particular politics. While many gender and sexuality scholars pay attention to intersectionality as a way to highlight multiple axes of oppression and disadvantage with a view to eradicating these, this approach may not always be relevant for gender nonconforming bottoms. Within the realm of a sex-positive approach to gay, bisexual and MSM sexual fantasy, it seems expedient to consider how intersectionality may be embodied and communicated in a range of ways and with multiple ends.

This chapter has sought to suggest some of the implications of effeminate belonging for sexual wellbeing among gay men. Sexual wellbeing shifts the discourse away from specific concerns around sexual health, which may not map easily onto non-Western settings where *gay* and *LGBTQ+* have limited appeal or reach, or which may only appeal to middle-class men exposed to Western perspectives. By contrast, sexual wellbeing connotes aspects such as sexual self-respect and self-esteem and the ways in which gay men might feel accepted or welcomed in their sexual and gendered identities. As a concept, sexual wellbeing is relevant in multiple spaces, not just healthcare ones. Sexual wellbeing is developed and contested in the body, in the home, in school and higher education, at work, online and in the various places and spaces people find themselves day to day.

Moreover, sexual wellbeing and belonging are contextual and may shift over time, place and space. I've also highlighted the need for a variety of professionals and practitioners to be open to the ways in which gay men or MSM may live according to a range of perspectives and sexual fantasy logics, some of which may contradict or at least challenge commonly accepted Western liberal suppositions concerning gender relations and sexual behaviour. Attending to narratives, whether fictional or non-fictional, can help professionals and practitioners develop sensitivity and the ability to suspend judgement when listening to stories and perspectives similar to those discussed in this book. Equally, there needs to be the cultural space in which such narratives can find expression in the first place. As ever, it comes down to asserting a variety of ways to be gay, and those fem bottoms who seek heterogender unions with masculine men are just as much entitled to belong in that gay space as are masculine men who seek each other for sexually versatile encounters.

CONCLUSION

It's hugely welcome that anal sex role positionality is now being taken seriously by scholars from a range of disciplinary backgrounds, especially for gay men who may feel that the nuances of their sex lives are often overlooked by those who ostensibly take an interest in them. And yet this book has shown that, while Anglo-American attempts to detach stereotypical gender expectations from anal sex role have been instrumental in tackling rigid stereotypes about 'masc tops' and 'fem bottoms', it remains the case that for some gay men, connections between effeminacy or gender nonconformity and bottoming are critical for identity formation.

Indeed, I've tried to show that attempts to negotiate gender expression and anal sex role preferences have implications for experiences of marginalisation and belonging, in multiple places and spaces. The narratives explored in this book demonstrate that in many cases, experiences of homophobia may be more accurately labelled experiences of *effeminophobia*, and that these can be experienced within LGBTQ+ spaces as well as non-LGBTQ+ ones.

And yet one of the most heartening discoveries I made while writing this book was the importance of creativity in responding to how one is 'read' by others. The significance of effeminophobia for sense of belonging seems to me to lie in the fact that questions of identity and meaning can all too easily rest predominantly in the hands of bullies and abusers. Being called names impacts how identity is formed, often well before one has tried to take charge of this independently. So, when a 'pansy boy' turns around and reclaims this label, planting pansies in places of woe, this represents a courageous feat of creative re-reading. And when a *tapette* seeks ownership of his narrative, he can explore possibilities for his sexual and gendered sense of self that places limits on early experiences of prejudice to define his future. Or, when a gay model chooses to resist the naysayers and re-imagine possibilities for being a 'faggy bottom', power dynamics are recalibrated, and hope seems possible.

Indeed, the narratives explored in this book highlight the porous boundaries between 'lived experience', which is assumed to be 'authentically' autobiographical and thus instils trust in listeners/readers, and the imaginative life narrative of possibility (Lejeune, 1989; Plummer, 1995). Effeminate belonging resists remaining at the level of trying to represent one's experience 'faithfully': it actively seeks to transform it through creative acts of re-reading, re-positioning and imagination. One might even ask whether a life narrative, especially one that explores experiences of marginalisation and prejudice, can ever be truly *faith*-full if it has not been allowed to flower into an imaginative re-telling that bestows agency on a teller in search of hope.

Creative responses, whether they be through poetry, documentary, drama, modelling, erotica, music or imagery, also underscore the sense that different modes of belonging and marginalisation intersect in personal experience. Belonging in the body seems tied up with belonging at home, school or in the LGBTQ+ community. Belonging in the LGBTQ+ community seems connected to belonging in the wider society. And belonging in the present is sometimes precariously connected to belonging to historical and transcultural identities, behaviours and forms of affiliation and ostracisation.

Power remains important in shaping people's identities and life narratives and the way they experience belonging and marginalisation, especially in their gendered and sexual forms (Plummer, 1995). But gender and sexuality cannot be reduced entirely to social and cultural influences shaping these aspects of the human condition (Norton, 2016). For the concept of embodiment to be genuinely useful in the humanities and social sciences, it needs to dialogue more fruitfully with the psychobiological, and the way people respond to the 'givenness' of their bodies, no matter how much these are also shaped by wider social, cultural and economic forces and expectations.

As such, this book has sought to triangulate currently fragmented research into gay men's sex roles and gender expression. Creative narratives can give voice to the ways in which people struggle to articulate meaning from their embodied experiences of gender and sexuality. But positivist studies in psychology and the human sciences can also offer tantalising glimpses into psychobiological patterns and tendencies that help generalise individual experience and therefore unite the self to others. In turn, knowledge of such influences can strengthen the imaginative search for meaning as these influences are lived out in the spaces and places of daily life.

Finally, how might the LGBTQ+ community respond to the challenge of effeminate belonging? Specifically, where does the effeminate bottom sit within Anglo-American gay communities that for decades have consistently marginalised such a figure from their consciousness? Historically and transculturally, beyond the current Anglo-American sphere of discourse, effeminate bottoms have been a central if albeit contested presence: recognised, sometimes welcomed, even desired. Often more visible as an ideal type than a neatly identifiable reality on the ground, gender nonconforming males who prefer receptive anal sex nevertheless represent a heterogenous but distinctive body within the wider gay community, as they always have done.

Such bottoms might be stigmatised, especially by a gay community that often finds connections between bottoming and effeminacy distasteful and politically inconvenient. But surely the answer isn't to pretend that fem bottoms don't exist, or that being a bottom has no connection whatsoever to gender nonconformity, at least for some. Surely the answer is to destigmatise such a combination and find ways to belong. In this book, I've tried to begin such a project by drawing attention to historical and cross-cultural exemplars where effeminacy and bottoming have been accepted as 'natural bedfellows'. From such a perspective, the relatively recent 'goals of the modern gay movement' in the West, which advocates 'a positive gay identity [that] attempts to free men from the tyranny of rigid role-playing', seem less self-evidently 'right' and universally applicable to all same-sex attracted males (Wooden & Parker, 1983, p. 145).

Language, history and representation matter. They can either work negatively, increasing experiences of marginalisation, loneliness and shame. Or they can be used more positively, harnessed to suggest avenues of belonging. It's through such avenues that we re-read ourselves and reconnect our lives, come to voice and find strength in knowing we are not, and never have been, alone.

ABOUT THE AUTHOR

Richard Vytniorgu is a Research Fellow in the School of Health and Social Work at the University of Hertfordshire, UK. A literary scholar by training, his interdisciplinary and comparative research focuses on sexual/gendered identities and belonging, place and inclusion, with expertise in narrative and autobiographical representation across different media and genres. He has also published widely on twentieth-century women's autobiographical writing, masculinity, philosophy of education and student belonging. His research has been supported by funding from the AHRC, ESRC and Wellcome Trust. Before joining Hertfordshire in 2023, he held academic posts at the University of Nottingham and University of Exeter and has worked on AHRC and ESRC-funded projects exploring historical and contemporary dimensions of LGBTQ+ belonging, loneliness and inclusion in Britain.

Twitter/X: @rvytniorgu

BIBLIOGRAPHY

PRIMARY TEXTS

Bandyopadhyay, M. (2010). Being male, being kothi. https://www.youtube.com/watch?v=N3qqWu296gw. Accessed on February 20, 2023.

Butterell, J. (dir.). (2021). *Everybody's talking about Jamie*. Regency Enterprises.

Cooper, V. (dir.). (2017). *Olly Alexander: Growing up gay*. Antidote Productions.

Feit, C. (2015). A woman in my heart. http://www.feitphoto.com/kothi. Accessed on February 20, 2023.

Fontaine, A. (dir.). (2017). *Reinventing Marvin*. Ciné-@.

Gabeu. (2019). Amor rural (clip oficial). https://www.youtube.com/watch?v=0U-CxqgzCPU. Accessed on December 1, 2023.

Harfleet, P. (2017). *Pansy boy*. Barbican Press.

Orrotica. (2016). SHORT: Seeds of a twink variety. https://www.gayspiralstories.com/story/show/20737. Accessed on February 20, 2023.

Porcel, J. (2018). *Samantha Hudson*. FILMIN.

Pup Don. (2021). Bimbo boys. https://www.gayspiralstories.com/series/show/10000678. Accessed on February 20, 2023.

Sivan, T. (2018). Bloom (official video). https://www.youtube.com/watch?v=41PTANtZFW0. Accessed on February 20, 2023.

Sivan, T. (2019). Lucky strike (official video). https://www.youtube.com/watch?v=-QsYn0j-7JQ. Accessed on February 20, 2023.

Sivan, T. (2021). Angel baby (official video). https://www.youtube.com/watch?v=IR-6KE8C4VQ. Accessed on February 20, 2023.

Stone, G. (2001). Pussyboy. http://eroticstories.menonthenet.com/index.cfm?m=article&ArticleRecId=294439. Accessed on February 20, 2023.

Solito, A. (dir.). (2005). *The blossoming of Maximo Oliveros*. Cinemalaya.

Xanderboy. (2008). From bear to fair (-y) (part 1). https://www.gayspiralstories.com/story/show/632. Accessed on February 20, 2023.

SECONDARY TEXTS

Ahmed, S. (2017). *Living a feminist life*. Duke University Press.

Alam, P., & Marston, C. (2023). 'People are having lots of other kinds of sex': Exploring sexual lifeworlds of LGBTQ+ young people in Bangladesh. *Cogent Social Sciences*, 9(1), 2185305.

Allan, J. A. (2016). *Reading from behind: A cultural analysis of the anus*. Zed Books.

Arnold, A. P. (2009). The organizational–activational hypothesis as the foundation for a unified theory of sexual differentiation of all mammalian tissues. *Hormones and Behavior*, 55, 570–578.

Arroyo, B. (2016). From flow to float: Moving through porn tube sites. *Porn Studies*, 3(3), 308–310.

Ayala, G., Makofane, K., Santos, G. M., Beck, J., Do, T. D., Hebert, P., Wilson, P. A., Pyun, T., & Arreola, S. (2013). Access to basic HIV-related services and PrEP acceptability among men who have sex with men worldwide: Barriers, facilitators, and implications for combination prevention. *Journal of Sexually Transmitted Diseases*, 2013.

Baer, B. J. (2005). Engendering suspicion: Homosexual panic in the post-Soviet detektiv. *Slavic Review*, 64(1), 24–42.

Bailey, J. M., & Zucker, K. J. (1995). Childhood sex-typed behavior and sexual orientation: A conceptual analysis and quantitative review. *Developmental Psychology*, 31(1), 43.

Baker, P. (2020). *Fabulosa! The story of Polari, Britain's secret gay language*. Reaktion Books.

Baker, P., & Stanley, J. (2003). *Hello Sailor! The hidden history of gay life at sea*. Longman.

Bao, A. M., & Swaab, D. F. (2011). Sexual differentiation of the human brain: Relation to gender identity, sexual orientation and neuropsychiatric disorders. *Frontiers in Neuroendocrinology*, *32*(2), 214–226.

Barker, M. (2014). The 'problem' of sexual fantasies. *Porn Studies*, *1*(1–2), 143–160.

Bartel, H. (2020). *Men writing eating disorders: Autobiographical writing and illness experience in English and German narratives*. Emerald Publishing Limited.

Bartlett, N. (1988). *Who was that man? A present for Oscar Wilde*. Serpent's Tail.

Bell, D., & Valentine, G. (Eds.). (1995). *Mapping desire: Geographies of sexualities*. Routledge.

Bereket, T., & Adam, B. D. (2006). The emergence of gay identities in contemporary Turkey. *Sexualities*, *9*(2), 131–151.

Bergling, T. (2001). *Sissyphobia: Gay men and effeminate behavior*. Harrington Park Press.

Bersani, L. (1987, October). Is the rectum a grave? *JSTOR*, *43*, 197–222.

Bollas, A. (2023). Men, sides, and homosexism: A small-scale empirical study of the lived experiences of men who identify as sides. *Journal of Homosexuality*, 1–13.

Boyce, P. (2007). 'Conceiving kothis': Men who have sex with men in India and the cultural subject of HIV prevention. *Medical Anthropology*, *26*(2), 175–203.

Brennan, J. (2016a). 'Bare-backing spoils everything. He's spoiled goods': Disposal and disgust, a study of retired power bottom twink Jake Lyons. *Porn Studies*, *3*(1), 20–33.

Brennan, J. (2016b). 'Shouldn't Tom Daley be a bottom?': Homosexual stereotyping online. *Sexualities*, *19*(7), 853–868.

Bristow, J. (1995). *Effeminate England: Homoerotic writing after 1885*. Columbia University Press.

Brody, E., Greenhalgh, S. P., & Sajjad, M. (2022). Gayservatives on Gab: LGBTQ+ communities and far right social media. *Social Media+ Society*, *8*(4).

Brooks, V. R. (1981). *Minority stress and lesbian women*. Lexington.

Brooks, T. R., Reysen, S., & Shaw, J. (2017). Smashing back doors in: Negative attitudes toward bottoms within the gay community. *World, 4*(2), 129–139.

Browne, K., Lim, J., & Brown, G. (Eds.). (2009). *Geographies of sexualities: Theory, practices and politics*. Ashgate Publishing.

Buchanan, L., & Ryan, K. J. (Eds.). (2010). *Walking and talking feminist rhetorics: Landmark essays and controversies*. Parlor Press LLC.

Butler, J. (2004). *Undoing gender*. Routledge.

Callahan, I., & Loscocco, K. (2023). The prevalence and persistence of homophobia in Italy. *Journal of Homosexuality, 70*(2), 228–249.

Cardoso, F. L. (2005). Cultural universals and differences in male homosexuality: The case of a Brazilian fishing village. *Archives of Sexual Behavior, 34*(1), 103–109.

Carrier, J. M. (1971). Participants in urban Mexican male homosexual encounters. *Archives of Sexual Behavior, 1*(4), 279–291.

Carrier, J. M. (1976). Cultural factors affecting urban Mexican male homosexual behavior. *Archives of Sexual Behavior, 5*, 103–124.

Carrier, J. M. (1977). 'Sex-role preference' as an explanatory variable in homosexual behavior. *Archives of Sexual Behavior, 6*(1), 53–65.

Carrillo, H. (1999). Cultural change, hybridity and male homosexuality in Mexico. *Culture, Health & Sexuality, 1*(3), 223–238.

Carrillo, H. (2002). *The night is young: Sexuality in Mexico in the time of AIDS*. University of Chicago Press.

Carrillo, H., & Fontdevila, J. (2014). Border crossings and shifting sexualities among Mexican gay immigrant men: Beyond monolithic conceptions. *Sexualities, 17*(8), 919–938.

Cavalcante, A. (2017). 'I did it all online': Transgender identity and the management of everyday life. *Critical Studies in Media Communication, 33*(1), 109–122.

Chauncey, G. (1994). *Gay New York: Gender, urban culture, and the making of the gay male world, 1890–1940*. Basic Books.

Cole, S. (2000). 'Macho man': Clones and the development of a masculine stereotype. *Fashion Theory, 4*(2), 125–140.

Crisp, Q. (1985). *The naked civil servant*. Flamingo.

D'Augelli, A. R., Grossman, A. H., & Starks, M. T. (2005). Parents' awareness of lesbian, gay, and bisexual youths' sexual orientation. *Journal of Marriage and Family, 67*, 474–482.

Daniele, M., Fasoli, F., Antonio, R., Sulpizio, S., & Maass, A. (2020). Gay voice: Stable marker of sexual orientation or flexible communication device? *Archives of Sexual Behavior, 49*, 2585–2600.

Davis, D. (2018, August 28). Troye Sivan talks about being a queer icon – And being labelled a bottom. *Them.* https://www.them.us/story/troye-sivan-bloom-interview. Accessed on February 20, 2023.

Dean, T. (2009). *Unlimited intimacy: Reflections on the subculture of barebacking.* University of Chicago Press.

DeVore, E. N. (2022). *Ambivalent sexism and condom use self-efficacy amongst men who bottom: A serial mediation model.* PhD Dissertation, University of Tennessee.

Dolezal, L. (2021). Shame, stigma and HIV: Considering affective climates and the phenomenology of shame anxiety. *Lambda Nordica, 26*, 47.

Dolezal, L. (2022). Shame anxiety, stigma and clinical encounters. *Journal of Evaluation in Clinical Practice, 28*(5), 854–860.

Duggan, L. (2002). The new homonormativity: The sexual politics of neoliberalism. *Materializing Democracy: Toward a Revitalized Cultural Politics, 10*, 175–194.

Dyer, R. (1985). Male gay porn: Coming to terms. *Jump Cut, 30*, 27–29.

Dyer, R. (1990). *Now you see it: Studies on lesbian and gay film.* Routledge.

Dynes, W. R. (1995). Queer studies: In search of a discipline. *Academic Questions, 8*(4), 34–52.

Eguchi, E. (2009). Negotiating hegemonic masculinity: The rhetorical strategy of 'straight-acting' among gay men. *Journal of Intercultural Communication Research, 38*(3), 193–209.

Epstein, S. (1987). Gay politics, ethnic identity: The limits of social constructionism. *Socialist Review, 17*, 9–51.

Farrell, R. A. (1972). The argot of the homosexual subculture. *Anthropological Linguistics, 14*(3), 97–109.

Felski, R. (2011). Context stinks! *New Literary History, 42*(4), 573–591.

Fenton, N. E., Shields, C., McGinn, M., & Manley-Casimir, M. (2012). Exploring emotional experiences of belonging. *Workplace: A Journal for Academic Labor*, (19).

Fernández-Alemany, M., & Murray, S. O. (2002). *Heterogender homosexuality in Honduras*. iUniverse.

Fiesler, C., & Proferes, N. (2018). 'Participant' perceptions of Twitter research ethics. *Social Media+ Society*, 4(1). https://doi.org/10.1177/2056305118763366

Florêncio, J. (2020). *Bareback porn, porous masculinities, queer futures: The ethics of becoming-pig*. Routledge.

Folkierska-Żukowska, M., Rahman, Q., & Dragan, W. Ł. (2022). Childhood gender nonconformity and recalled perceived parental and peer acceptance thereof, internalized homophobia, and psychological wellbeing outcomes in heterosexual and gay men from Poland. *Archives of Sexual Behavior*, 51(4), 2199–2212.

Formby, E. (2017). *Exploring LGBT spaces and communities: Contrasting identities, belongings and wellbeing*. Routledge.

Freud, S. (1975). *Three essays on the theory of sexuality* (James Strachey, Trans.). Basic Books.

Galeano, J. F. (2022). Mariquitas, 'marvellous race created by God': The judicial prosecution of homosexuality in Francoist Andalusia, 1955–70. *Journal of Contemporary History*, 57(3), 775–801.

Galvão, C. A. (2022, September 26). Challenging traditional sertanejo, Brazil's Gabeu creates space for queer love songs. *npr*. https://www.npr.org/2022/09/26/1124383971/challenging-traditional-sertanejo-brazils-gabeu-creates-space-for-queer-love-son. Accessed on December 1, 2023.

Garcia, J. N. C. (2009). *Philippine gay culture: Binabae to bakla, silahis to MSM*. Chicago University Press.

Garcia-Rabines, D. (2022). Love in the gay world: Negotiating intimate relationships in Lima's middle-class gay Scene. *Journal of Homosexuality*, 69(6), 1097–1118.

Geraths, C. (2022). Anthos, bottoms, and anal sex in Troye Sivan's 'Bloom'. In J. Rhodes & J. Alexander (Eds.), *The Routledge handbook of queer rhetoric* (pp. 258–264). Routledge.

Gerrard, B., Morandini, J., & Dar-Nimrod, I. (2023). Gay and straight men prefer masculine-presenting gay men for a high-status role: Evidence from an ecologically valid experiment. *Sex Roles*, *88*(3–4), 119–129.

Gill, H. (2016). Kothi. In A. Wong, et al. (Eds.), *The Wiley Blackwell encyclopedia of gender and sexuality studies*. Wiley-Blackwell.

Glick, P., Gangl, C., Gibb, S., Klumpner, S., & Weinberg, E. (2007). Defensive reactions to masculinity threat: More negative affect toward effeminate (but not masculine) gay men. *Sex Roles*, *57*, 55–59.

Gómez Jiménez, F. R., Court, L., & Vasey, P. L. (2021). Occupational preferences and recalled childhood sex-atypical behavior among Istmo Zapotec men, women, and muxes. *Human Nature*, *32*(4), 729–747.

Gorman-Murray, A. (2008). Reconciling self: Gay men and lesbians using domestic materiality for identity management. *Social & Cultural Geography*, *9*(3), 283–301.

Gorman-Murray, A., & Cook, M. (Eds.). (2020). *Queering the interior*. Routledge.

Green, R. (1987). *The 'sissy boy syndrome' and the development of homosexuality*. Yale University Press.

Green, A. V. (2020, April 27). Getting to the bottom of topping stereotypes: How gay sex became vulnerable to outdated hetero gender roles. *Xtra Magazine*. https://xtramagazine.com/love-sex/gay-sex-stereotypes-bottoming-topping-170667. Accessed on September 20, 2022.

Greenhalgh, S. P., Koehler, M. J., Rosenberg, J. M., & Willet, K. B. S. (2020). Considerations for using social media data in learning design and technology research. In *Research methods in learning design and technology* (pp. 64–77). Routledge.

Grieg, J. (2020, March 16). A brief history of bottoming. *Vice*. https://www.vice.com/en/article/qjdnep/gay-bottom-history-lgbtq-culture. Accessed on February 16, 2023.

Guasch, O. (2011). Social stereotypes and masculine homosexualities: The Spanish case. *Sexualities*, *14*(5), 526–543.

Gubrium, J. F., & Holstein, J. A. (1997). *The new language of qualitative method*. Oxford University Press.

Guitoo, A. (2021). 'Are you gay or do you do gay?' Subjectivities in 'gay' stories on the Persian sexblog shahvani. com. *Asiatische Studien-Études Asiatiques, 75*(3), 881–899.

Halperin, D. M. (1990). *One hundred years of homosexuality and other essays on Greek love*. Routledge.

Halwani, R. (1998). Essentialism, social constructionism, and the history of homosexuality. *Journal of Homosexuality, 35*(1), 25–51.

Harfleet, P. (2015). The pansy project. *Contemporary Theatre Review, 25*(3), 424–425.

Harry, J. (1983). Defeminization and adult psychological wellbeing among male-homosexuals. *Archives of Sexual Behavior, 12*(1), 1–19.

Hekma, G. (2014). Queer Amsterdam 1945–2010. In J. V. Evans & M. Cook (Eds.), *Queer cities, queer cultures: Europe since 1945* (pp. 118–134). Bloomsbury.

Hekma, G., Oosterhuis, H., & Steakley, J. (1995). Leftist sexual politics and homosexuality: A historical overview. *Journal of Homosexuality, 29*(2–3), 1–40.

Hennen, P. (2001). Powder, pomp, power: Toward a typology and genealogy of effeminacies. *Social Thought & Research, 24*(1/2), 121–144.

Hennen, P. (2008). *Faeries, bears, and leathermen: Men in community queering the masculine*. University of Chicago Press.

Hinchman, L., & Hinchman, S. (Eds.). (2001). *Memory, identity, community: The idea of narrativity in the human sciences*. New York University Press.

Hines, M. (2011). Prenatal endocrine influences on sexual orientation and on sexually differentiated childhood behavior. *Frontiers in Neuroendocrinology, 32*(2), 170–182.

Hoppe, T. (2011). Circuits of power, circuits of pleasure: Sexual scripting in gay men's bottom narratives. *Sexualities, 14*(2), 193–217.

Hoskin, R. A. (2019). Femmephobia: The role of anti-femininity and gender policing in LGBTQ+ people's experience of discrimination. *Sex Roles, 81*, 686–703.

Houlbrook, M. (2005). *Queer London: Perils and pleasures in the sexual metropolis, 1918–1957*. Chicago University Press.

Hunt, C. J., Fasoli, F., Carnaghi, A., & Cadinu, M. (2016). Masculine self-presentation and distancing from femininity in gay men: An experimental examination of the role of masculinity threat. *Psychology of Men & Masculinity*, *17*(1), 108.

Janion, L. (2022). 'Homosexual men whose lives turned out unsuccessful': Polish aunties in the transition era. *Text and Performance Quarterly*, *42*(3), 332–345.

Janssen, D. F. (2017). Karl Heinrich Ulrichs: First theorist of erotic age orientation. *Journal of Homosexuality*, *64*(13), 1850–1871.

Jennings, T. W. (2005). *Jacob's wound: Homoerotic narrative in the literature of ancient Israel*. Continuum.

Johnson, K. L., Gill, S., Reichman, V., & Tassinary, L. G. (2007). Swagger, sway, and sexuality: Judging sexual orientation from body motion and morphology. *Journal of Personality and Social Psychology*, *93*(3), 321.

Jones, A. (2019). Sex is not a problem: The erasure of pleasure in sexual science research. *Sexualities*, *22*(4), 643–668.

Jones, C., & Vytniorgu, R. (2022). *The beat of our hearts: staging new histories of LGBTQIA+ loneliness and belonging*. https://blogs.exeter.ac.uk/beatofourhearts/files/2022/04/The-Beat-of-Our-Hearts-A5-Report-Digital-Final.pdf. Accessed on February 17, 2023.

Kaiser, T., Del Giudice, M., & Booth, T. (2020). Global sex differences in personality: Replication with an open online dataset. *Journal of Personality*, *88*, 415–429.

Kemp, J. (2013). *The penetrated male*. Punctum Books.

Kennedy, U., & Maguire, E. (2018). The texts and subjects of automediality. *M/C Journal*, *21*.

Kort, J. (2020, May 28). Side guys: Thinking beyond gay male "tops" and "bottoms". *Psychology Today*. https://www.psychologytoday.com/us/blog/understanding-the-erotic-code/202005/side-guys-thinking-beyond-gay-male-tops-and-bottoms. Accessed on February 16, 2023.

Kulick, D. (1997). The gender of Brazilian transgendered prostitutes. *American Anthropologist*, *99*(3), 574–585.

Kulick, D. (1998). *Travesti: Sex, gender and culture among Brazilian transgendered prostitutes*. University of Chicago Press.

Kutner, B. A., Simoni, J. M., Aunon, F. M., Creegan, E., & Balán, I. C. (2021). How stigma toward anal sexuality promotes concealment and impedes health-seeking behavior in the US among cisgender men who have sex with men. *Archives of Sexual Behavior, 50,* 1651–1663.

Lähdesmäki, T., Saresma, T., Hiltunen, K., Jäntti, S., Sääskilahti, N., Vallius, A., & Ahvenjärvi, K. (2016). Fluidity and flexibility of "belonging" Uses of the concept in contemporary research. *Acta Sociologica, 59*(3), 233–247.

Lambevski, S. A. (1999). Suck my nation-masculinity, ethnicity and the politics of (Homo) sex. *Sexualities, 2*(4), 397–419.

Lehavot, K., & Lambert, A. J. (2007). Toward a greater understanding of antigay prejudice: On the role of sexual orientation and gender role violation. *Basic and Applied Social Psychology, 29*(3), 279–292.

Lejeune, P. (1989). In P. J. Eakin (Ed.), *On autobiography* (Katherine Leary, Trans.). University of Minnesota Press.

LeVay, S. (1994). *The sexual brain.* The MIT Press.

LeVay, S. (1996). *Queer science: The use and abuse of research into homosexuality.* The MIT Press.

LeVay, S. (2017). *Gay, straight, and the reason why: The science of sexual orientation.* Oxford University Press.

Levine, M. P. (1998). *Gay macho: The life and death of the homosexual clone.* New York University Press.

Li, G., Kung, K. T., & Hines, M. (2017). Childhood gender-typed behavior and adolescent sexual orientation: A longitudinal population-based study. *Developmental Psychology, 53,* 764–777.

Lippa, R. A. (2020). Interest, personality, and sexual traits that distinguish heterosexual, bisexual, and homosexual individuals: Are there two dimensions that underlie variations in sexual orientation? *Archives of Sexual Behavior, 49*(2), 607–622.

Loftin, C. M. (2007). Unacceptable mannerisms: Gender anxieties, homosexual activism, and swish in the United States, 1945–1965. *Journal of Social History, 40*(3), 577–596.

Lyons, A., & Hosking, W. (2014). Health disparities among common subcultural identities of young gay men: Physical, mental, and sexual health. *Archives of Sexual Behavior, 43,* 1621–1635.

Maddison, S. (2015). Is the queen dead? Effeminacy, homosociality and the post-homophobic queer. *Key Words: A Journal of Cultural Materialism, 13*, 39–56.

Maki, J. (2017). Gay subculture identification: Training counselors to work with gay men. *Vista Group Counseling*. https://nsuworks.nova.edu/cps_facarticles/1822. Accessed on February 21, 2024.

Maldonado, L. G. (2021, December 4). Samantha Hudson: 'Nunca anunciaría bancos ni eléctricas; Soy una asalariada pero con ética'. *El Español*. https://www.elespanol.com/porfolio/entrevistas/20211204/samantha-hudson-nunca-anunciaria-bancos-electricas-asalariada/1002525827394_33.html. Accessed on February 20, 2023.

Manalansan, M. F. (2003). *Global divas: Filipino gay men in diaspora*. Duke University Press.

May, V., & Muir, S. (2015). Everyday belonging and ageing: Place and generational change. *Sociological Research Online, 20*(1), 72–82.

McCormack, M. (2012). *The declining significance of homophobia: How teenage boys are reclaiming masculinity and heterosexuality*. Oxford University Press.

McGill, C. M., & Collins, J. C. (2015). Creating fugitive knowledge through disorienting dilemmas: The issue of bottom identity development. *New Horizons in Adult Education and Human Resource Development, 27*, 29–40.

McKee, A. (2014). Humanities and social scientific research methods in porn studies. *Porn Studies, 1*(1–2), 53–63.

Mercer, J. (2017). *Gay pornography: Representations of sexuality and masculinity*. Bloomsbury.

Meyer, I. H. (1995). Minority stress and mental health in gay men. *Journal of Health and Social Behavior*, 38–56.

Miles, C. C., & Terman, L. (1936). *Sex and personality: Studies in masculinity and femininity*. McGraw-Hill Book Company.

Milton, J. (2022, February 8). The long, deep, surprisingly versatile history of bottoms: From Ancient Greece to modern misogyny. *Pink News*. https://www.thepinknews.com/2022/02/08/bottoming-history-gay-bottoms/. Accessed on February 16, 2023.

Montclaire State University LGBTQ+ Center. (n.d.). Terminology. https://www.montclair.edu/lgbtq-center/lgbtq-resources/terminology/. Accessed on February 16, 2023.

Moser, C. (2019). 2.7 Automediality. In M. Wagner-Egelhaaf (Ed.), *Handbook of autobiography/autofiction* (pp. 247–261). De Gruyter.

Moskowitz, D. (2022). Spotlight feature: Born to bottom. In *Gender and sexuality development: Contemporary theory and research* (pp. 518–521).

Moskowitz, D. A., & Garcia, C. P. (2019). Top, bottom, and versatile anal sex roles in same-sex male relationships: Implications for relationship and sexual satisfaction. *Archives of Sexual Behavior*, 48(4), 1217–1225.

Mousley, A. (2013). *Literature and the human: Criticism, theory, practice*. Routledge.

Mowlabocus, S. (2010). *Gaydar culture: Gay men, technology and embodiment in the digital age*. Routledge.

Msibi, T., & Rudwick, S. (2015). Intersections of two isiZulu genderlects and the construction of skesana identities. *Stellenbosch Papers in Linguistics Plus*, 46, 51–66.

Muñoz, J. E. (2019). Cruising Utopia: The then and there of queer futurity. In *Cruising Utopia* (10th Anniversary Ed.). New York University Press.

Murray, S. O. (1989). Homosexual acts and selves in early modern Europe. *Journal of Homosexuality*, 16(1–2), 457–477.

Murray, S. O. (1995). *Latin American homosexualities*. University of New Mexico Press.

Murray, S. O. (1996). *American gay*. University of Chicago Press.

Murray, S. O. (2000). *Homosexualities*. University of Chicago Press.

Nardi, P. M. (1998). The globalization of the gay & lesbian socio-political movement: Some observations about Europe with a focus on Italy. *Sociological Perspectives*, 41(3), 567–586.

Neves, S., & Davies, D. (Eds.). (2023). *Relationally queer: A pink therapy guide for practitioners*. Routledge.

Nguyen, T. H. (2014). *A view from the bottom: Asian American masculinity and sexual representation*. Duke University Press.

Norton, R. (2010). F*ck Foucault: How eighteenth-century homosexual history validates the essentialist model. https://rictornorton.co.uk/fuckfouc.pdf. Accessed on January 24, 2022.

Norton, R. (2016). *The myth of the modern homosexual: Queer history and the search for cultural unity*. Bloomsbury Academic.

Ntuli, P. M. (2009). *IsiNgqumo: Exploring origins, growth and sociolinguistics of an Nguni urban-township homosexual subculture*. Doctoral Dissertation. https://researchspace.ukzn.ac.za/server/api/core/bitstreams/e7cd191e-cc25-43ea-90c2-a0db32118e64/content

Odets, W. (2020). *Out of the shadows: Reimagining gay men's lives*. Picador.

O'Flynn, B. (2018, May 16). The complicated politics of the twink. *i-D Magazine*. https://i-d.vice.com/en_uk/article/evkdjp/the-complicated-politics-of-the-twink. Accessed on October 20, 2021.

Oleksiak, T. (2022). On taking the bottom's stance, or not your typical submissive. In J. Rhodes & J. Alexander (Eds.), *The Routledge handbook of queer rhetoric* (pp. 357–363). Routledge.

Paasonen, S. (2011). *Carnal resonance: Affect and online pornography*. The MIT Press.

Paasonen, S. (2018). Elusive intensities, fleeting seductions, affective voices. *Porn Studies*, 5(1), 27–33.

Palmer, P. (1993). *To know as we are known: Education as a spiritual journey*. HarperOne.

Parker, R. (1999). *Beneath the equator: Cultures of desire, male homosexuality, and emerging gay communities in Brazil*. Routledge.

Pascoe, C. J. (2012). *Dude, you're a fag: Masculinity and sexuality in high school*. University of California Press.

Person, E. S., & Ovesey, L. (1984). Homosexual cross-dressers. *The Journal of the American Academy of Psychoanalysis*, 12(2), 167–186.

Phoenix, C. H., Goy, R. W., Gerall, A. A., & Young, W. C. (1959). Organizing action of prenatally administered testosterone propionate on the tissues mediating mating behavior in the female guinea pig. *Endocrinology*, 65, 369–382.

Pile, S. (2010). Emotions and affect in recent human geography. *Transactions of the Institute of British Geographers*, 35, 5–20.

Piontek, T. (2006). *Queering gay and lesbian studies*. University of Illinois Press.

Plummer, D. (1963). *Queer people: The truth about homosexuals in Britain*. W. H. Allen.

Plummer, K. (1995). *Telling sexual stories: Power, change and social worlds*. Routledge.

Poletti, A., & Rak, J. (2014). *Identity technologies: Constructing the self online*. University of Wisconsin Press.

Powles, A. (2003). Dance of the dedicated bottom. In R. Reynolds & G. Sullivan (Eds.), *Getting it!: Gay men's sexual stories* (pp. 109–117). Haworth Press.

Prieur, A. (1998). *Mema's house, Mexico City: On transvestites, queens, and machos*. University of Chicago Press.

Rabarison, K. (2014, December 1). Woman in my heart: Candace Feit. *The Morning News*. https://themorningnews.org/gallery/woman-in-my-heart. Accessed on February 20, 2023.

Ravenhill, J. P., & de Visser, R. O. (2017). Perceptions of gay men's masculinity are associated with their sexual self-label, voice quality and physique. *Psychology & Sexuality*, 8(3), 208–222.

Ravenhill, J. P., & de Visser, R. O. (2018). "It takes a man to put me on the bottom": Gay men's experiences of masculinity and anal intercourse. *The Journal of Sex Research*, 55(8), 1033–1047.

Ravenhill, J. P., & de Visser, R. O. (2019). "I don't want to be seen as a screaming queen": An interpretative phenomenological analysis of gay men's masculine identities. *Psychology of Men & Masculinities*, 20(3), 324.

Reddy, G. (2001). Crossing 'lines' of subjectivity: The negotiation of sexual identity in Hyderabad, India, South Asia. *Journal of Southeast Asian Studies*, 24, 91–101.

Reilly, A. (2016). Top or bottom: A position paper. *Psychology & Sexuality*, 7(3), 167–176.

Reilly, A., Yancura, L. A., & Young, D. M. (2013). Three predictive variables of social physique anxiety among gay men. *Psychology & Sexuality*, 4(3), 244–254.

Richardson, N. (2009). Effeminophobia, misogyny and queer Friendship: The cultural themes of Channel 4's Playing It Straight. *Sexualities, 12*(4), 525–544.

Richlin, A. (1993). Not before homosexuality: The materiality of the cinaedus and the Roman law against love between men. *Journal of the History of Sexuality, 3*(4), 523–573.

Rios, L. F., Paiva, V., & Brignol, S. (2019). Passivos, ativos and versáteis: Men who have sex with men, sexual positions and vulnerability to HIV infection in the Northeast of Brazil. *Culture, Health & Sexuality, 21*(5), 510–525.

Rohr, R. (2019). *Things hidden: Scripture as spirituality.* SPCK.

Sánchez, F. J., & Vilain, E. (2012). Straight-acting gays': The relationship between masculine consciousness, anti-effeminacy, and negative gay identity. *Archives of Sexual Behavior, 41*, 111–119.

Sanders, T., du Plessis, C., Mullens, A. B., & Brömdal, A. (2023). Navigating detransition borders: An exploration of social media narratives. *Archives of Sexual Behavior, 52*(3), 1061–1072.

Sandfort, T. G. (2005). Sexual orientation and gender: Stereotypes and beyond. *Archives of Sexual Behavior, 34*(6), 595–611.

Sandfort, T. G., Melendez, R. M., & Diaz, R. M. (2007). Gender nonconformity, homophobia, and mental distress in Latino gay and bisexual men. *The Journal of Sex Research, 44*(2), 181–189.

Santoro, P. (2016). Lather, rinse, reclaim: Cultural (re) conditioning of the gay (bear) body. In R. M. Boylorne & M. P. Orbe (Eds.), *Critical autoethnography* (pp. 159–175). Routledge.

Sarson, C. (2020). 'Hey man, how's u?': Masculine speech and straight-acting gay men online. *Journal of Gender Studies, 29*(8), 897–910.

Savic, I., Garcia-Falgueras, A., & Swaab, D. F. (2010). Sexual differentiation of the human brain in relation to gender identity and sexual orientation. *Progress in Brain Research, 186*, 41–62.

Schatzberg, A. F., Westfall, M. P., Blumetti, A. B., & Birk, C. L. (1975). Effeminacy. I. A quantitative rating scale. *Archives of Sexual Behavior, 4*, 31–41.

Schleifer, R., & Vannatta, J. B. (2019). *Literature and medicine.* Springer International Publishing.

Schofield, K., & Schmidt, R. (2005). Fashion and clothing: The construction and communication of gay identities. *International Journal of Retail & Distribution Management*. https://doi.org/10.1108/09590550510593239

Sedgwick, E. K. (1991). How to bring your kids up gay. *Social Text*, 29(1), 18–27.

Shaw, A., & Sender, K. (2016). Queer technologies: Affordances, affect, ambivalence. *Critical Studies in Media Communication*, 33(1), 1–5.

Signorile, M. (1997). *Life outside: The Signorile report on gay men: Sex, drugs, muscles, and the passages of life*. Harper Collins Publishers.

Sinfield, A. (1994). 'Effeminacy' and 'femininity': Sexual politics in Wilde's comedies. *Modern Drama*, 37(1), 34–52.

Smith, S., & Watson, J. (2010). *Reading autobiography: A guide for interpreting life narratives*. University of Minnesota Press.

Smyth, R., Jacobs, G., & Rogers, H. (2003). Male voices and perceived sexual orientation: An experimental and theoretical approach. *Language in Society*, 32(3), 329–350.

Snapes, L. (2019, April 6). Troye Sivan: 'I have to get comfortable with being effeminate'. *Guardian*. https://www.theguardian.com/fashion/2019/apr/06/troye-sivan-youtuber-singer-actor-fashion-queer-pride-laura-snapes. Accessed on February 20, 2023.

Stief, M. (2017). The sexual orientation and gender presentation of Hijra, Kothi, and Panthi in Mumbai, India. *Archives of Sexual Behavior*, 46(1), 73–85.

Stines, S. (2017). Cloning fashion: Uniform gay images in male apparel. *Critical Studies in Men's Fashion*, 4(2), 129–151.

Suire, A., Tognetti, A., Durand, V., Raymond, M., & Barkat-Defradas, M. (2020). Speech acoustic features: A comparison of gay men, heterosexual men, and heterosexual women. *Archives of Sexual Behavior*, 49, 2575–2583.

Swift, J. (2018, June 22). Years in the making. *The Sun*. https://www.thesun.co.uk/tvandshowbiz/6595490/years-and-years-difficult-second-album-tour-interview/. Accessed on February 20, 2023.

Swift-Gallant, A., Coome, L. A., Aitken, M., Monks, D. A., & VanderLaan, D. P. (2019). Evidence for distinct biodevelopmental influences on male sexual orientation. *Proceedings of the National Academy of Sciences*, 116(26), 12787–12792.

Swift-Gallant, A., Coome, L. A., Monks, D. A., & VanderLaan, D. P. (2017). Handedness is a biomarker of variation in anal sex role behavior and recalled childhood gender nonconformity among gay men. *PloS One*, *12*(2), e0170241.

Swift-Gallant, A., Di Rita, V., Major, C. A., Breedlove, C. J., Jordan, C. L., & Breedlove, S. M. (2021). Differences in digit ratios between gay men who prefer receptive versus insertive sex roles indicate a role for prenatal androgen. *Scientific Reports*, *11*(1), 8102.

Tasos, E. (2022). To what extent are prenatal androgens involved in the development of male homosexuality in humans? *Journal of Homosexuality*, *69*(11), 1928–1963.

Taywaditep, K. J. (2002). Marginalization among the marginalized. *Journal of Homosexuality*, *42*(1), 1–28.

Thing, J. (2009). *Entre maricones, machos, y gays: Globalization and the construction of sexual identities among queer Mexicanos*. PhD Dissertation, University of Southern California.

Thoma, B. C., Eckstrand, K. L., Montano, G. T., Rezeppa, T. L., & Marshal, M. P. (2021). Gender nonconformity and minority stress among lesbian, gay, and bisexual individuals: A meta-analytic review. *Perspectives on Psychological Science*, *16*(6), 1165–1183.

Thomas, H. (2017). *Sissy!: The effeminate paradox in postwar US literature and culture*. University of Alabama Press.

Tomori, C., Srikrishnan, A. K., Ridgeway, K., Solomon, S. S., Mehta, S. H., Solomon, S., & Celentano, D. D. (2018). Perspectives on sexual identity formation, identity practices, and identity transitions among men who have sex with men in India. *Archives of Sexual Behavior*, *47*, 235–244.

Tripp, C. A. (1977). *The homosexual matrix*. Quartet Books.

Trumbach, R. (1998). *Sex and the gender revolution, volume 1: Heterosexuality and the third gender in enlightenment London*. University of Chicago Press.

Underwood, S. G. (2003). *Gay men and anal eroticism: Tops, bottoms, and versatiles*. Routledge.

VanderLaan, D. P., Skorska, M. N., Peragine, D. E., Coome, L. A., Moskowitz, D. A., Swift-Gallant, A., & Monks, D. A. (2022). Carving the biodevelopment of same-sex sexual orientation at its joints. In *Gender and sexuality development: Contemporary theory and research* (pp. 491–537). Springer International Publishing.

Vasey, P. L., & VanderLaan, D. P. (2014). Evolving research on the evolution of male androphilia. *The Canadian Journal of Human Sexuality, 23*(3), 137–147.

Vidal-Ortiz, S., Decena, C., Carrillo, H. G., & Almaguer, T. (2009). Revisiting activos and pasivos: Towards new cartographies of Latino/Latin American male same-sex desire. In *Latina/o sexualities: Probing powers, passions, practices, and policies* (pp. 253–273). Rutgers University Press.

Vytniorgu, R. (2019). *The butterfly hatch: literary experience in the quest for wisdom: Uncanonically seating H.D.* Liverpool University Press.

Vytniorgu, R. (2023). Effeminate gay bottoms in the West: Narratives of pussyboys and boiwives on Tumblr. *Journal of Homosexuality, 70*(10), 2113–2134.

Vytniorgu, R. (2024a). Coming to voice as total top or total bottom: Autobiographical acts and the sexual politics of versatility on Reddit. *Journal of Homosexuality*. https://doi.org/10.1080/00918369.2024.2307544

Vytniorgu, R. (2024b). Twinks, fairies, and queens: An historical inquiry into effeminate gay bottom identity. *Journal of Homosexuality, 71*(7), 1605–1625.

Wallien, M. S., & Cohen-Kettenis, P. T. (2008). Psychosexual outcome of gender-dysphoric children. *Journal of the American Academy of Child & Adolescent Psychiatry, 47*(12), 1413–1423.

Warner, M. (2002). *Publics and counterpublics.* Princeton University Press.

Watson, C. (2012). Analysing narratives: The narrative construction of identity. In S. Delamont (Ed.), *Handbook of qualitative research in education* (pp. 460–473). Edward Elgar.

Waugh, T. (1996). *Hard to imagine: Gay male eroticism in photography and film from their beginnings to Stonewall.* Columbia University Press.

Weatherhead, S. (2011). Narrative analysis: An often overlooked approach. *Clinical Psychology Forum, 218*, 47–52.

Weinrich, J. D., Grant, I., Jacobson, D. L., Robinson, S. R., McCutchan, J. A., & HNRC Group. (1992). Effects of recalled childhood gender nonconformity on adult genitoerotic role and AIDS exposure. *Archives of Sexual Behavior, 21*, 559–585.

Whitam, F. L. (1980). The prehomosexual male child in three societies: The United States, Guatemala, Brazil. *Archives of Sexual Behavior, 9*, 87–99.

Wignall, L. (2022). *Kinky in the digital age: Gay men's subcultures and social identities*. Oxford University Press.

Williams, L. (1989). *Hard core: Power, pleasure and the frenzy of the visible*. University of California Press.

Williams, R. (2003). *Television: Technology and cultural form*. Routledge.

Williams, C. (2010). *Roman homosexuality*. Oxford University Press.

Winder, T. J. (2023). Assume the position: Bottom-shaming among black gay men. In D. Berkowitz, et al. (Eds.), *Male femininities* (pp. 262–278). New York University Press.

Wooden, W. S., & Parker, J. (1983). *Men behind bars: Sexual exploitation in prison*. Da Capo Press.

Worthen, M. G. (2024). Anti-femininity or gender-nonconformity prejudice? An investigation of femme, twink, and butch LGBTQ victimization using norm-centered stigma theory. *Critical Criminology*, 1–19.

Young, M. (1999). *King James VI and I and the history of homosexuality*. Palgrave Macmillan.

Young, M. B. (2021). *King James and the history of homosexuality*. Fonthill.

Zane, Z. (2021, July 15). What is a power bottom? Here's what the sex term really means. *Men's Health*. https://www.menshealth.com/sex-women/a37023996/power-bottom-definition/. Accessed on February 16, 2023.

Zuger, B. (1988). Is early effeminate behavior in boys early homosexuality? *Comprehensive Psychiatry, 29*(5), 509–519.

Zwicky, A. (2018, August 14). Butch fagginess. *Arnold Zwicky's Blog*. https://arnoldzwicky.org/2018/08/14/butch-fagginess/. Accessed on February 16, 2023.

Zwicky, A. (2019, October 16). Adventures in homomasculinity: The pink jock. *Arnold Zwicky's Blog*. https://arnoldzwicky.org/2019/10/16/adventures-in-homomasculinity-the-pink-jock/. Accessed on February 16, 2023.

Zwicky, A. (2022, March 25). Nelly and Nancy. https://arnoldzwicky.org/2022/03/25/nelly-and-nancy/. Accessed on June 28, 2023.

INDEX

Activational effects, 44
Africa, 35–36
Agropoc (music genre), 87–88
Alexander, Olly, 9–10, 78–83, 86–87, 118
Anal sex role
   positionality, 125
   preference, 2, 7
Anal warts, 42–43
Androgens, 45
Androphilia, 27–28
Angel Baby, 60–61, 86
Anglo-American gay communities, 126–127
Archives of Sexual Behavior, 7
Argentina, 62
Ariano model, 97
Author positionality, 9–11
Autobiographical acts, 58
Autobiography, 62–63
Automediality, 62–63

Bakla, 10, 45, 74–75
Bar Addison model, 95–96, 100–101
BDSM/kink, 33, 107–108, 112
BDSMLr, 122
Beautiful On the Outside (2019), 78
Beautiful People, 69–70
Being Male, Being Kothi, 60, 89–90
BelAmi, 61–62
Belonging, 126
   connection to marginalisation, 44

definitions of, 41–44
in different places and spaces, 44–53
embodiment, 44–47
family, home and school, 47–49
LGBTQ+/Gay 'Community', 49–52
online spaces, 52–53
politics of, 84
scholarly treatment of, 82
to stigmatised identity, 53–55
Bersani, Leo, 8
Bicha, 5, 10
Bimbo Boys, 101–102, 120
Blasé, 24–25
Blazing faggot, 45
Blossoming of Maximo Oliveros, The, 59, 74
Body image /type, 31
   considerations of, 31
Boiwife, 107, 112, 120–121
Bottom, 42, 118
   definitions of, 1–2
   as disposable and detachable label, 83–92
   historical examples of, 2
   as identity, 83–84
   scholarly treatment of, 12
   as sexual role, 35
   transcultural expressions of, 2
Bottom fag, 62
Bottom identities
   Bakla, 10, 45, 74–75
   Bicha, 5, 10
   Boiwife, 107, 112, 120–121
   Catamite, 26

Cinaedus, 42–43
Ciota, 35–36
Fag/faggot, 5, 10, 45, 52–53, 62, 106, 119
Faggy bottom, 30, 33
Fairy, 3, 27, 35, 95, 104, 110
Femboy, 110
Jota, 35–36
Kothi, 36, 87–88, 93, 118–119
Kūnī, 37
Loca, 10, 110
Lubunya, 37
Marica/mariquita, 82, 98–100
Maricón, 27
Paneleiro, 36–37
Pansy/pansy boy, 3, 31, 35, 60, 69–71, 74, 76
Pasivo/passive, 96–97, 100
Pocpoc, 37
Poof, 3, 35, 45, 106
Power bottom, 30, 33
Pussyboy, 62, 105, 107, 112, 120–121
Queen/quean, 3–5, 31, 95, 97, 104, 110
Queer, 26–27, 100
Sissy boy, 47, 77, 110
Skesana, 35–37
Tapette, 5, 10, 45, 125
Twink, 31, 93–94, 116, 118
Viado, 35–36
Weibling/weichling, 34
Bottom queens, 33
BoyfriendTV, 53, 94
Brazil, 35–37, 87–88
Britain, 3, 26–27, 36, 50, 77
Butch fagginess, 32–33
Butch shift, 30–31, 50
Butler, Judith, 46

Camp, 24–25
Carnal resonance, 13, 114
Carrier, Joseph M., 36, 96

Catamite, 26
Chauncey, George, 26–27, 30–31, 34–35, 49, 102, 105
Cinaedi, 42–43
Cinaedus, 42–43
Clones, 50
Clothing, 8, 77, 79, 90, 103–104
Cocky Boys, 61–62
Comfort with sexuality, 116
Coming Up For Air (2021), 78
Creative narratives, 126
Creative responses, 126
Crisp, Quentin, 49–51

Daddy, 110–111
  connection to masculinity, 111
  as identity, 84–85
Daley, Tom, 10, 31, 78
Dallas Preston model, 95–96
Data Lounge, 61
Dating Amber, 76
Defeminisation, 69–76
Deviation of sexual aim, 34
Deviation of sexual object, 34
Documentaries, 60
  discussions of, 30
Doonan, Simon, 65

Education, 122–123
Effeminacy, 7, 23, 25, 69, 76
  connection to gender nonconformity, 8–9
  deep structures, 23–29
  defeminising, 71
  definitions of, 7
  gay voice/mannerisms, 10, 24–25, 47
  historical examples of, 4
  as identity, 4
  in relation to trans, 10–11, 18, 46, 81, 114
  scholarly treatment of, 12
  transcultural expressions of, 27
Effeminacy Scale, 24
Effeminate, 62

Index

Effeminate belonging, 1–2, 8, 27–28, 60, 125–126
   language of, 44
Effeminate bottom, 69
Effeminate fag, 62
Effeminate gay man (EGM), 42
Effeminophobia (*see also* Femmephobia), 43, 125
Egalitarian homosexuality, 3–4, 38, 50, 112
Embodiment, 44, 47, 126
End of Eddy, The, 72
Erotic narratives, 61–65
Erotica
   discussions of, 57
   online nature of, 52–53
Ethnicity, considerations of, 123
Everybody's Talking About Jamie (2021), 47–48, 59–60, 76

Fag, 10, 45, 119
Faggot, 5, 52–53, 62, 106, 119
Faggy, 24, 95
Faggy bottoms, 30, 33
Fairy, 3, 27, 35, 95, 104, 110
FamilyDick, 94
Feit, Candace, 61, 89–90
Fem bottoms, 93, 125
   belonging, 112–114
   model, 93–101
   writing and desiring, 101–107
Fem gay bottom, 2
   bottom as disposable and detachable label, 83–92
   gender displaced, 69–76
   sexual orientation and triumph of gay, 76–83
Fem gays, 61–62
Femboy, 110
Femininity, 25
Feminist-inspired critical writing, 12
Femmephobia(*see also* Effeminophobia), 43
Film, discussions of, 6, 64–65

Flaming queens, 24
Foucault, Michel, 26
France, 59
Freud, Sigmund, 29–30, 34–35
Gabeu (Gabriel Silva Felizardo), 60–61, 87–88, 90
Ganymede, 26
Gay, 4, 96, 115
Gay bottom identities, 23
   deep structures, 23–29
Gay culture, 104–105
Gay men, 1, 42, 93–94
Gay porn
   discussions of, 61
   online nature of, 14
   paratexts, 84
   scholarship on, 61
Gay Pornography: Representations of Sexuality and Masculinity, 61
Gay sensibility, 3–4
Gay Spiral Stories, 101, 104, 107, 123
Gay voice, 24–25, 47
Gender expression, 2, 5, 29, 38
Gender identity, 23–24, 49
Gender nonconformity, 7, 23, 41–42, 95
   as an experience
   deep structures, 23–29
   definitions of
Genderqueer, 23–24, 32–33
Geographies of sexualities, 8, 44
Green, Richard, 47–48
Guardian, 87

Haemorrhoids, 42–43
Harfleet, Paul, 73, 83, 90, 117
Hennen, Peter, 25–26
Heterogender homosexuality, 4
Hirschfeld, Magnus, 34
Home, 8, 46–47, 49, 108, 111, 123
Homophile, 3, 45
Homophobia, 41–42, 47–48, 60, 79–80, 125

Homosexual identity, 10–11, 35
Houlbrook, Matt, 5–6, 50, 102
Hudson, Samantha (Iván Gonzalez Ranedo), 60, 81
Hunk, 94

Identity, 11
   connection to narrative, 6
   sexual identity, 44
India, 35–37, 88
Ingle, 26
Internacional Latin American discourses, 3
Invert, 35
Iran, 35–36, 106
It's a Sin, 59

Journal of Homosexuality, 7
Journal of Sex Research, 7

Kothi, 36, 87–88, 93, 118–119
Kulick, Don, 2, 17, 109
kūnī, 37

Latin America, 110–111, 118–119
Leo Grand model, 95–96
LeVay, Simon, 28–29
LGB, 115
LGBTQ+ community, 18, 126–127
LGBTQ+ counsellors, 121
LGBTQ+ media, 1
'LGBTQ+/Gay 'Community', 49–52
Liveable life, 46
Loca, 10, 110
Loquita, 97
Lubunya, 37
Lucas Entertainment, 94
'Lucky Strike', 60–61

M2M Club, 62, 99–100, 119
Macho, 96
Machos, 100
Male homosexuality, 26
Mannerisms, 8, 45, 64, 75–76, 94, 98, 102–104

Marginalisation, 41–44
Marica, 10, 119
Maricas, 110
Maricon, 45
Mariquita, 82
Masc tops, 125
masc4masc, 95–96, 101, 120
Masculine gay man (MGM), 42
Masculinity
   cultural dimensions of, 119–120
   importance of, 14
   lack of, 1
   psychobiological explanations of, 45, 95
Maximo Oliveros, 75–76
Mediterranean, 38, 42, 119
Men Behind Bars: Sexual Exploitation in Prison (Wooden and Parker), 3
Men who have sex with men (MSM), 115
Methodological considerations, 11–14
Middle-class homosexuals, 3, 34–35, 50
Minority stress, 41–42
Moderno Latin American discourses, 3
Murray, Stephen O., 26, 53–54, 112

Naked Civil Servant, The (1985), 49
Narratives, 57, 69
   autobiographical, 58
   erotic and pornographic, 61–65
   importance of, 60
   non-erotic, 59–61
   reading of, 6
Nelly, 24–25, 33, 95
Nelly queen, 118
Next Door Twink, 94
Non-Anglophone languages, 2
Non-erotic narratives, 59–61

Non-western gender-nonconforming bottoms, 35–38
Non-Western labels, 2–3
Non-Western localities, 2
Norton, Rictor, 25–26, 90–91

Olly Alexander: Growing Up Gay (Alexander), 9, 60, 78
Online erotica, 52–53
Online spaces, 52–53
OnlyFans, 53
Organisational effects, 44
Out of the Shadows: Reimagining Gay Men's Lives (Odets), 3–4

Paasonen, Susanna, 13, 64
Paneleiros, 36–37
Pansy, 3, 31, 35
Pansy Boy (2017), 60, 69–71, 74, 76
Paratextual, 13–14
Pasivo, 96–97, 100
Passive fag, 62
Pathic, 26
Personal homosexual identity, 27
Place and space, 124
Poc, 37, 88
Polari, 37
Poof, 3, 35, 45, 106
Porn 2.0, 61
Porn Studies, 61
Pornographic narratives, 61–65
Pornography, 52–53
Power, 126
  bottom, 30, 33
Pre-exposure prophylaxis (PrEP), 115
Prenatal hormone theory of sexual orientation, 28
Proud (2015), 79–80
Purposeful wandering, 58
Pussyboy, 62, 105, 107, 112, 120–121

Queens, 3–5, 31, 95, 97, 104, 110
Queer theory, 6
Queernejo, 87–88

r/TopsAndBottoms, 63
Receptive Anal Intercourse (RAI), 29
Reddit, 52–53, 61
Reinventing Marvin (2017), 47, 59, 64, 71–74, 76, 119–120
RuPaul's Drag Race, 14–15
Rural spaces, 60–61, 88
Ryan Evans model, 95–96

School, 8, 47, 49
Scientific enquiry, 11–12
Sean Cody, 61–62
Sedgwick, Eve Kosofsky, 43
Self-awareness, 11
Sex object choice, 5, 29, 38
Sex role, 29–38
Sexual Brain, The (1994), 29
Sexual career, 2–3
Sexual complementarity, 3
Sexual health to sexual wellbeing, 115–117
Sexual orientation, 76–83
Sexual self-esteem, 116
Sexual self-respect, 116
Sexual wellbeing, 115
  bodies, expectations and environmental context, 117–124
  definitions of, 115
  importance for effeminate belonging, 115
  sexual health to, 115–117
Sexuality
  definitions of, 2
  psychobiological explanations of, 14
Sexually transmitted infection (STI), 115
'SHORT: Seeds of a Twink Variety', 120
Sissy, 10, 45, 62, 119

Sissy boys, 47, 110
Sissyphobia, 43
Sivan, Troye, 60–61, 85–86, 118
Sociability, 58
Social media, 10, 52
South Africa, 35–36
Southern Strokes, 94
Spain, 60
Steelers, 105–106
Steelers: The World's First Gay Rugby Club (2020), 79–80
Stereotypical effeminacy, 24
Stigma
  attached to bottoming, 41
  attached to effeminacy, 29
Subjectivity, 89
Swishes, 3, 24–25
Swishy, 24

Tannor Reed model, 95–96, 100–101
Tapette, 5, 10, 45, 125
Three Essays on the Theory of Sexuality (1905), 34
To Be a Gay Man (2020), 78
Top, 3, 34

Trans, 18, 46–47, 81, 114
Transcultural types of effeminate bottoms, 27
Transhistorical types of effeminate bottoms, 27
Triumph of gay, 76–83
Tumblr, 52–53, 63, 108, 122
Twink, 31, 93–94, 116, 118
Twitter/X, 52–53, 63, 122

Ulrichs, Karl Heinrich, 34
United States, 35, 41–42

Weiblings, 34
Weichling, 34
Weinrich, James D., 27–29
Western labels, 2–3
Woman in My Heart, A, 61
Working-class, 2–3, 5–6, 35

XHamster, 53, 94
XVideos, 53, 94

Zwicky, Arnold, 32–33